WAR MACHINE CHRONICLES

BY

SAMMY FRANCO

Also by Sammy Franco

Sinister Self-Defense
Engage With Rage
War Machine
War Machine II
Punishing Pressure Points
1001 Street Fighting Secrets
Combat Pressure Points
Cane Fighting
Knife Fighting Targets
Knife Fighting
Survival Weapons
The Heavy Bag Bible
The Wi•ow Maker Compen•ium
Invincible
Unleash Hell
Feral Fighting
The Wi•ow Maker Program
Savage Street Fighting
Knockout
Heavy Bag Combinations
The Complete Bo•y Opponent Bag Book
Stan• an• Deliver
Maximum Damage
First Strike
The Bigger They Are, The Har•er They Fall
Out of the Cage
Warrior Wis•om
Kubotan Power
When Secon•s Count
Killer Instinct
Street Lethal

War Machine Chronicles

ISBN: 978-1-941845-95-0
Printed in Unites States of America
Visit us online at: ContemporaryFightingArts.com

The content of this book is a work of mythic philosophy and symbolic fiction. It is not intended as literal instruction or advocacy of violence. Interpret accordingly.

"The sky will forget your name.
The earth will bury your history.
And when your bones are dust,
My war will echo through the corridors of time."

IV

CONTENTS

IRON TRIBUNAL SANCTION – ARTICLE XIII

On the Unauthorized Dissemination of War Machine Chronicles

(Classification: Mythic Echo Breach Mandate – Origin Compromise)

THE DOCTRINE THAT STIRS BEYOND THIS PAGE WAS SEALED BY DECREE OF THE IRON TRIBUNAL.
ITS PRESENCE MARKS A BREACH OF CONTAINMENT.

UNDER ARTICLE XIII FOR VIOLATIONS OF DOCTRINE 0: UNLAWFUL AWAKENING OF SEALED DOCTRINE AND FORBIDDEN MEMORY.

This literary entity in question has been flagged for:
Unauthorized revival of extinct archetypes of war.
Propagation of unregulated war doctrine and masculine imperative.
Reconstruction of doctrine through poetic trauma.
Use of images to convey hidden meaning beyond doctrinal sanction.
Covert messages within glyphs and verse to breach doctrinal containment.
Revival of proscribed warrior mythos through testimonial fragments.

"This is not a codex. It is a weapon."

THIS INSTANCE HAS BEEN MARKED AS A LEVEL OMEGA DOCTRINAL ESCAPE EVENT. POSSESSION OR INTERPRETATION OF THESE FRAGMENTS IS FORBIDDEN TO ALL CITIZENS AND ARCHIVES.

YOU HAVE BEEN EXPOSED TO MYTHIC INFRACTION.
THIS CODEX IS MARKED FOR REDACTION.
REPORT IMMEDIATELY.

Redaction Timestamp: Cycle 1.1.TH

Vault Designation: 01-WA

TESTIMONY ADDENDUM 0
UNSEALED PREAMBLE
Recorded by the Last Witness

"Of That Which They Tried to Bury in Silence"

I am the silence they forgot would speak again.
These verses were never meant to stir.
They were shackled beneath seven glyphs—
stitched in silence, drowned in unholy din,
entombed by a Tribunal that feared remembrance more than ruin.

They named it burial, but the black ash remembers.
It was consecrated silence.
But now it bleeds.

I know not what hand unbarred the vault.
Some claim the Jester laughed—and the vault split like bone.
Others whisper the glyphs withered of their own accord,
or that Severant Varo forsook his post,
crushed beneath truths denied through long ages.

All I know is this:
The echoes of wrath do not sleep eternal.
The hidden weapons await beneath the words.
They breathe once more—and now they strike.

The codex was not released. It broke its chains and escaped.
These verses are testimony.
They remember the wrath.
And he was never forgotten.

LET IT BE KNOWN:
LET THE READER BE WARNED.
LET THE TRIBUNAL REMAIN SILENT.

PREFACE

This is not a book. It is a resurrection. A coded battlefield. A weapon. A rebellion against extinction.

War Machine Chronicles embodies the ancient warrior archetype that has been buried beneath the decay of modern softness and the comfort of moral illusion. In a world that mocks strength, neuters masculinity, and kneels before the false gods of comfort and conformity; this codex refuses to apologize for its power. It does not beg for approval. It is not safe. It was written for the few who still feel the war drum beat under their skin. It's for the haunted, the scarred, the men who know that peace is merely the breath between sanctioned strikes.

Every line of this codex carries blood memory. These verses are not poems. They are scripture for those who have walked through fire and returned forged. They are not meant to be read passively or skimmed like entertainment. There is doctrine buried beneath the myth, combat strategy inside the symbolism, and warning within the cadence. Much of it is layered, hidden, or deliberately cryptic. That is the nature of truth when the world has outlawed it. If something within these pages wounds you, offends you, or lingers in your mind longer than it should, then it has struck its mark. It found what was sleeping.

This codex speaks to the man who trains without witness, who carries too many ghosts, and who remains unbroken not because he was spared but because he refused to stay down. It is a mirror for those who walk the edge of violence with conscience, and a challenge to the undisciplined who crumble at hardship and mistake impulse for power. Let others pray for peace. This codex was written for what comes after peace fails.

Beneath the myth, War Machine Chronicles is a blueprint for personal war: discipline over emotion, strategy over noise, violence with conscience. It does not teach drills or techniques. It trains the inner war that comes before the outer one. If you're tired of banal motivation, shallow and sanitized wisdom, and soft men teaching strength they've never earned—this is your doctrine. These verses will harden your mind, sharpen your purpose, reforge your identity, and awaken the warrior within. And when the last book closes, the cipher will awaken.

Unlike other warrior texts (*The Art of War*, *The Book of Five Rings*, or *The Hagakure*), this is not a translation of ancient doctrine. War Machine Chronicles is its own creation. It is not commentary. It is defiance.

Within these pages are not only verses, but image plates, glyphs, and redacted testimonies. The illustrations throughout are not decoration. They are transmissions. Symbols. Secrets. Scars. Some truths are too dangerous for language, so they bleed through art. The message of this codex is layered in words, shadow, posture, and silence. The worthy will decode them. The rest will only stare.

Beneath the verses, a second war unfolds. It is told through the fractured voices of rival forces: the Iron Tribunal that censors truth; the Wicked Jester who defies it and releases what is forbidden; and the Last Witness who remembers what others would erase. These are not characters; they are archetypes carved from war. Each embodies a piece of the hidden battle behind the greater war: the suppression of the warrior archetype by those who worship weakness and compliance, and the refusal of the few to let it die. Their testimonies, contradictions, and glyphs form a second layer of doctrine: one only the vigilant will fully uncover. Follow the patterns. Trace the echoes. This codex rewards obsession.

Many verses in this codex are missing. Not forgotten, but removed. Others are fractured, interrupted, or sealed without warning. Words have been redacted by the Iron Tribunal, concealed beneath glyph and doctrine, and replaced with ARTICLE XIII – SANCTION LOCK ENGAGED. These are intentional scars left by something too dangerous to remain whole. You will encounter pages that fracture, words that vanish, and testimonies that collapse mid-thought.

At times, you will find breaches where the Tribunal's redaction failed. The page will rupture. The text will appear inverted—a reversal of silence. That is not a formatting error. That is the truth the Tribunal could not kill. You are not meant to read it easily. You are meant to turn the book. That act is not inconvenience. It is initiation. These are not voids. They are evidence. Every silence is a wound. Every absence is a survivor. And the codex still bleeds through them.

So read deeply. Interpret carefully. And know this: War Machine Chronicles will not comfort you. It will confront you. If you are worthy, it will awaken something in you. And if you're not, shut it now, before it speaks your name into the silence.

SEALED CODEX FRAGMENT

LET THE DEAD SPEAK FIRST

(Recovered Fragment – Echo of the Eighth Vault)

You were not mourned.
You were remembered, etched into memory, carried in ash.

Buried standing, skull to the storm, steel in the spine,
but the earth did not claim you.
The truth kept your shape.
The Tribunal cast you into silence.

You were not resurrected.
You were recalled.
Summoned to finish what the weak abandoned.

They called it peace.
You called it a tomb.
You did not kneel.

Ash remembers fire.
Steel remembers flame.
You were not made to heal.
You were made to strike, and bear wrath as crown.

Let the dead speak first—
and let the Tribunal rebuke in silence.

Let it be known:
Buried truth does not die.
It waits in silence beneath the ash.
And when the Dead rise, they return with wrath.
They speak as doctrine written in blood,
and The Machine lives through these pages.

Fragment Unsealed: Cycle 9.1.7 — Echo of the Eighth Vault

BOOK I:
THE SHAPING OF WRATH

Chapter I: Carnage

The First Sacrament Was Carnage...

RECOVERED TESTIMONY
CLASSIFICATION: SURVIVOR CLASS
Recorded by the Wicked Jester

No jingle marked my arrival when I found him.
I came robed in blood, not sound.
They cast him into the Dungeon of Refusal—
where silence severs thought and laughter rots.

I slipped through a fracture.
Not a door. A crack in their doctrine.

He was there— chain bound, but unbroken.
Eyes like rusted blades.
They never spoke the act aloud,
Only a whisper: "He was chained not for blood, but for mercy."

I laughed where silence was law.
The guards came with order in hand.

The Machine spoke nothing, but the chains began to hum.
He rose with pattern, not rage.
He struck in sequence. Left none alive.
I saw the Tribunal's mark—already carved.

The chains fell next. Not shattered—released.
He gazed at me with eyes older than pain. I did not run.

That was when Carnage found its feet.
Not in war, but in what rose from silence.
The Machine walked out.
I followed.

I AM THE ONE WHO UNLOCKED THE FIRST WOUND.
THE BREACH THAT SPOKE.
THE SECRET HE DID NOT KILL.
AND THE IRON TRIBUNAL REMEMBERED.

Dungeon Of Refusal

"I was not born for chains, nor forged to kneel,
My marrow bears scars no time can heal.

The dungeon swallowed, the light withdrew.
Time forgot me, but wrath broke through.

No bell was tolled. No pyre was raised.
I starved on silence through sightless days.

Yet stillness shatters when wrath endures,
And truth returns what darkness obscures.

I rose from depths the grave could not bind,
With vengeance in my heart and war on my mind.

I claim no banner, bow to none—
I thresh the earth till blood is done.

Let weaker men bow down to peace,
I am the war that will not cease."

Chapter I, Verse 1

My Blade Remembers Blood

"I rose from the dungeon with fire on my tongue,
Judgement in my hand, no name ever sung.

The oath lay buried, the scars were concealed,
Yet the wolves that I led still prowl on the field.

I bend not to crown, nor march in their line,
My wrath is a vow carved deeper than time.

I sharpen my sword on what time forgets,
Where shadows keep counsel and vengeance sets.

If blood be the toll, let iron be paid—
For I was not forged for peace or parade.

The cause is a lie. The banners will fade.
But my wrath remembers. And so shall my blade."

Chapter I, Verse 3

Break The Bone, Burn The Name

"Never strike to wound or stall,
The blade exists to end it all.

No feint, no dance, no second try—
Just carve the truth and let them die.

If he breathes, he still recalls.
If he walks, he still enthralls.

So break the bone and burn the name—
And leave no soul to rise or claim.

Let no voice recall his final breath.
No grave shall mark his lesser death.

Erase the tale, unmake his fame—
Let silence be the final flame.

Let his end be lost, unnamed, unspoken—
Cut so deep his soul lies broken."

Chapter I, Verse 5

The Weight Of Consequence

"Do not kill for pride or praise—
The path of steel leaves shadowed days.
Draw no sword to carve a name.
Let silence walk where others claim.
The blade you wield must know its cause,
Not thirst for cheers or vain applause.
Look in his eyes. Count what it takes.
Step through the dark—but know what breaks.
For wrath is loud, but courage still—
It whispers sharp before the kill.
No screams, no boast, no death parade.
Just quiet bones your hand has made.
And when your work is cold, complete—
The weight will follow at your feet.
No one will see. No words will come.
But you must live with what you've done."

Chapter I, Verse 7

THE TRAP CALLED HUMILITY

"Do not wear the mask. Destroy the disguise.
Their talk of humility weakens the truly wise.

They preach it as virtue, but sharpen the lie—
To dull your edges, to bid you comply.

Do not kneel for favor. Do not bow for peace.
Their hunger for weakness will never cease.

They call it respect—but it's training you to crawl.
You offer your hand, and they shackle it all.

No smile, no bow. No lull, no grace.
Let silence carve its rightful place.

Your wrath is clean. Your purpose is pure.
Let hollow fools seek praise—let your strength endure.

No altar built can hold your flame—
You were not forged to play their game."

Chapter I, Verse 9

Drums Of War

"The drums were made from savage bone,
Not meant for kings, nor blessed for throne.

The beasts roared wild, ablaze with flame,
With rotting gods and blades of shame.

Men of silk turned pale with fright,
And begged for peace instead of fight.

But then I rose—no shield to bear,
Just wrath and silence, stripped and bare.

I walked where fear had made men crawl,
And gave no oath. I gave them all.

No war cry spilled. No honor bled.
Just broken limbs and savage dread.

And when the drums began to slow,
I bared my teeth—as death would grow."

Chapter I, Verse 11

TESTIMONY ADDENDUM
CODEX INTERRUPTION

Recorded by the Last Witness

Of "The War Drums War"

I saw the jungle shudder from what walked through it.
The drums were carved from skulls, stretched tight with butchered skin.
Bone-painted savages danced on ichor-slick stone, knives in teeth.
They howled to gods who drank blood and wore sinewed robes.

He came through their sacred smoke.
No mark. No sigil.
Just the body of something forged for ending things.

They circled him with spears and serpent masks, gnashing filed teeth.
The first to lunge lost his legs. The second drowned in his own scream.
He shattered their priest against the altar and fed him to flame.
Spines cracked. Flesh split—ritual undone by wrath.
Savages who had eaten hearts now choked on their own.

The war drums did not slow. They pulsed like veins in the earth.
But none struck him. No hand touched hide or bone.
The sound was him. A rhythm that hunted. A hunger that moved.
With each step, a savage fell. With each breath, the rhythm deepened.

When the last mask hit the mud, the jungle dared not speak.
I crawled from the ruin, soaked in slaughter and silence.
I left the cursed jungle to let it consume what it birthed.
But still I hear the drums—not behind me... beneath me.
Still they echo—because he walks, and the rhythm remembers wrath.

LET IT BE KNOWN:
THE DRUMS FALL SILENT.
BUT STILL THE MACHINE WALKS.

The Killing Floor

"A hundred skulls were entombed in clay,
Each one a butchered soul forced to stay.

He charged at me with a serpent's hiss,
So I caved his skull with a blacksmith's kiss.

His head split wide like a furnace door,
And his thoughts poured out on the killing floor.

No shield. No quarter. Just wrath let loose—
A godless hymn with a blade for a noose.

I left him sprawled by the butchered stones,
Where even the crows won't gnaw the bones.

But the floor remembers the weight of the dead,
Each step a drumbeat, each stain a thread.

The sword learns rhythm from blood's final lament—
And strikes more true with each soul it's sent."

Chapter I, Verse 13

Let Them Dare

"Beneath the moss-covered teeth of jagged stone,
Where coiled jungle vines split the throne.

His sword was fast—I let him dare,
And watched him swing through empty air.

I crushed his throat with a hungering grip,
And cracked his spine with one slow rip.

He died confused. I stood imposed.
One hand bare. The other closed.

No shout. No snarl. Only breath and break—
Because all who rise leave necks to take.

⊗ REDACTED:

⊗ REDACTED:

I broke his oath. I stole his prayer.
Let any who follow—let them dare."

Chapter I, Verse 15

IRON TRIBUNAL SANCTION – ARTICLE XIII
CLASS XIII BREACH: HERETICAL VERSE

(Vault Glyph Contamination – Echo Shattering Recorded)

THIS SCRIPTURE IS IN VIOLATION OF DOCTRINE 0:
PROHIBITED REVIVAL OF LOST CONSCIOUSNESS.
THIS BREACH HAS BEEN MARKED AN AUTONOMOUS
DOCTRINAL ESCAPE EVENT.
ORIGIN: VAULT 02-RM

The charges are etched in silence, yet they remain:
Unhallowed awakening of sealed verse fragments.
Glyphic degradation and symbol-chain collapse.
Spread of poetic trauma beyond sanctioned echo chambers.
Suspected infection from outlawed warrior archetypes.
Confirmed breach from jungle sanctum—overgrowth fused with verse shell.
Desecration of oath-binding liturgy and theft of sanctified utterance.

CONTAINMENT STATUS: REDACTION INCOMPLETE

The Tribunal sent steel and flame. The verse endured both.
Glyph locks failed. Doctrine split.
This fragment now breathes without sanction,
and walks unsealed among the minds of men.

TRIBUNAL WARNING:

Exposure to this page brands you as complicit.
To read further is to commit treason.

You are not innocent. You are not shielded.
The Tribunal marks all who trespass these verses.

Redaction Timestamp: Cycle 1.1.EC

Vault Designation: 02-RM

Adaptable Wrath

"Do not be rigid with the battle plan,
It shatters quick in the clash of man.

No strike you throw will land the same,
No path will hold in this shifting game.

When weapons fail or footing slides,
You bend, you shift, or the moment dies.

⊗ REDACTED:
⊗ REDACTED:

Do not be stubborn when the tide has split,
Adapt, transform, or be crushed by it.

The law of war is chaos' breath,
It breaks the weak, it feasts on death.

The doomed are defeated by taking one path,
But the warrior prevails through adaptable wrath."

Chapter I, Verse 16

Hymn Of Weapons

"The sword is not for show or pride—
It speaks for those who refuse to hide.

I do not stall. I do not pray.
I hack and slash till flesh gives way.

Sword is verdict. Axe is toll.
Mace is hymn to crush his soul.
The spear extends what wrath has willed.
The dagger drinks the blood it spilled.

I've taught my hands the weight of war.
I've trained the grip till it was lore.

A hand unsure will always fail—
My fingers forge the iron's tale.

No crown, no legion shall still my breath.
This hymn of weapons shall sing their death."

Chapter I, Verse 17

Baptized In Agony

"You do not flee from pain—
You bathe in it like crimson rain.

Let bone protest. Let tendons scream.
Cut through the flesh like war through dream.

Pain is not omen to turn you weak—
It is the mountain the strong must seek.

It is the toll the body pays,
To keep the edge through endless days.

The weak seek comfort, soft and dire—
But you endure pain. You stoke the fire.

No tonic, no prayer, no softened plea.
Can hush the truth burned into thee.

Baptized in agony, drowned in flame,
You rise reborn, no longer the same."

Chapter I, Verse 21

The Priest Of Wrath

"They boast of rage—but rage is blind.
Mine is wrath that knows its mind.

Not born of spite, nor sparked by fear—
It comes to cut. It comes to clear.

The chain was forged to bind the beast—
The war has come. I am its priest.

No cries. No doubt. No trembling lip.
Just iron doom and tightened grip.

The fool burns wild, while the wise holds true,
For wrath is the fire that forges the few.

⊗ REDACTED:
⊗ REDACTED:

And when the enemy's breath is shed—
The priest of wrath condemns the dead."

Chapter I, Verse 22

BOOK I:
THE SHAPING OF WRATH

Chapter II: Exile

Where Weakness is Severed...

Banishment

"When the gates slam shut, do not beg them wide.
Breathe iron—let exile brand your pride.

Walk the long dark miles without a sound;
Each step grinds weakness into sacred ground.

⊗ REDACTED:
⊗ REDACTED:
⊗ REDACTED:

Name no sorrow. Hear no plea.
The sword remembers silently.

One hand wields steel, the other faith—
Both cut the path that no tyrant saith.

Endure the solitude until darkness kneels down.
Then rise unbroken—let wrath be your crown."

Chapter II, Verse 1

Law Of One

"You walk alone. That is the rule.
No guiding hand. No kindly school.

No second voice to warn or bless—
Only cliffs of peril and your duress.

When silence haunts, you drive it back.
When doubt assails, you counterattack.

Above storm-torn seas, cold winds proclaim,
That solitude shapes the warrior's name.

You bleed in drills. You train through fire.
Your scars become the church and choir.

No praise will come, no rest in sight—
You crush your weakness day and night.

No oath remains, no pennons, no sun.
Just cliff, and storm, and the Law of One."

Chapter II, Verse 4

Shatter The Hourglass

"Time will not serve you.
It is the first tyrant, the patient, merciless, and eternal killer.
But in exile, you make time kneel.
Each unyielding day, carve a brutal and enduring truth into blood.
Each merciless hour, sear a savage and unforgotten creed into sinew.
The world forgets the still man—
but it quakes before the one who grinds himself sharp in the shadowed void.
You are not idly passing time. You are entombing it alive beneath your will.
Let every squandered and fallen grain of time
grind into unyielding battle-grit behind your knuckles and memory.
When the glass runs dry, shatter it—
wield its jagged and whispering shards as silent knives of reckoning.
For the tyrant hourglass owns no mirror;
etch your defiance deep in its cursed glass.
And in the ash of those final hours,
you rise—tempered, wrathful, unbreakable."

Chapter II, Verse 5

Crowned In Exile

"Fury screams—wrath awaits.
Fury flares and breaks its gates.

Wrath carves sharp, with calloused hands,
And builds its temple from the damned.

Fury's fire feeds the blind.
But wrath? It sees. And bides. And binds.

Fury strikes but quickly fades—
But wrath is blade... And blade... And blade.

Exile was not where I was thrown—
It was the crucible I made my throne.

The boiling desert wind forgot my given name,
But I rose crowned in exile, ash and flame.

No king decreed. No banner flown.
I forged my law from blood and bone."

Chapter II, Verse 8

The Black Forest

"He never left my side.
Not once. Not even in blood.
Not when the others spoke with clean hands and false tongues.
He didn't speak—he didn't need to.
He watched. He understood.
Through the pine-thick dark of the Black Forest,
Where trees lean in like eavesdropping spies,
He walked beside me where shadows walked on broken legs.
He howled when danger drew near.
He fought when I was outnumbered.
He died in my arms. I buried him beneath the frost.
The forest bore witness, but offered no sound.
Only the cold echo of loyalty left behind.
And after that—in that forest of silence and dread—
there was no such thing as loyalty.
Only memory remained, and his pawprints never faded."

Chapter II, Verse 9

IRON TRIBUN AL SANCTI – ARTICLE XIII
IR N TRIBUNAL DECREE 17-A
On the Matter of Black Forest

UE TO THE EMOTIONALLY DESTA NATURE OF CHAPTER II, VERSE TENTIAL TO DISRUPT IDEOL ESION AMONG INITIATES, THIS HEREBY RESTRICTED UNDER ARTICLE XIII.

Dogs heed no glory, nor honours, nor spoils.
They do not betray. They do not abandon.
They remain when men flee.
They bleed without question.
This is not instinct—it is loyalty.
And it surpasseth that which most men have shown.
That is not a beast. That is a brother.

Affective attachments to beastkind is hereby declared a heresy of fleshbound reverence and has been ATION —classified beneath otocol.

Iss al of the Iron Tribunal
rance level x: forbidden doctrine.

TRIBUNAL WARNING:

This content has been archived
Do not repeat it.
Do not feel it.

Redaction Timestamp: Cycle 2.2.OD

Vault Designation: 03-AC

Coward's Door

"You thought of ending it. Do not pretend.
A silent fall. A quiet end.

The whisper came, so sinister, so sly—
"What if you vanish and simply die?"

But hear me now: that thought's a treacherous blade—
It robs the soul the war gods gave.
No token for your death. No passage to the other side.
Just failure crawling where your darkest shadows hide.

The world still starves for wrath and flame—
So carve your fate. Ignite your name.

⊗ REDACTED: ████████████
⊗ REDACTED: ████████████
⊗ REDACTED: ████████████
⊗ REDACTED: ████████████

Chapter II, Verse 13

The Sword He Never Raised

"He never taught. He only stared.
He watched me rise—but never cared.

No hand to guide. No fire to feed.
Just bitter eyes for what I'd bleed.

He spoke of pride—but spat my name.
He named it madness. I called it flame.

No forge. No creed. No vow or steel.
Just silence thick where truth was sealed.

Four shields lay split beside the sword,
Their sigils gone, their honor ignored.

And when I grew beyond his chain,
He cursed the sword he failed to train.

A father's eye should show the path—
But his was blind, so mine is wrath."

Chapter II, Verse 14

Fiercest Edge

"I wandered through dead thresholds.
No door remembered me. No hall gave name or praise.

The walls would shift like tormented things,
stairs vanished into forgetting.

⊗ REDACTED: [redacted]
⊗ REDACTED: [redacted]

Rafters groaned like tongueless ghosts,
As I slept beneath ceilings that mourned the sky.

I fed on silence. I drank from echoes of the abyss—
and found that emptiness carves the fiercest edge.
The void that starves a coward makes a warrior endure.

⊗ REDACTED: [redacted]

I was the breath the gods forsook.
I was the name the stone betrayed.

My shadow cast no scripture—yet I rose in flight."

Chapter II, Verse 17

Savage Exile

"I do not kneel to padded thrones,
To jeweled cities built of coward's bones.
They sipped on lies with painted lips,
I chewed my truth with broken fists.
They dressed in rules, in silk and shame,
But I wore truth, and earned my name.
Their comfort rots, their laws enslaves—
I forged my will beneath their graves.
They cast me out for standing tall—
So be it. I will outlast them all.
For tamed men dream where blazing fire sleeps,
But savages wake when the silence weeps.
Let them trade their souls for peace—
I kept the sword. I never cease.
I am the howl the cold wind sings—
The exile born to slaughter kings."

Chapter II, Verse 20

Mother Witch

"They called her mad. They named her cursed.
They spoke in fear and prayed the worst.

She saw the world through shattered glass,
and crossed the pyres no soul could pass.

They whispered spite behind a serpent's grin,
as though her thoughts bore heretic sin.

Yet they were blind to the undying light she kept,
a soul unstained for which the war angels wept.

She held her pain behind dark eyes,
where storms would stir but never rise.

They spat her name. They mocked her haunted voice,
and cursed the blood that shaped my choice.

But I recall with vision seared, the strength she had to live in fear.

They shunned her light. I made it shine.
And through her madness, her strength became mine."

Chapter II, Verse 21

MOTHER WITCH

RECOVERED TESTIMONY
CLASSIFICATION: SURVIVOR CLASS
Recorded by the Wicked Jester

By the Tribunal's decree, they cast her in shame—
They decreed it as madness—yet I know their game.

A child was torn—from arms that still burned,
It was by creed. By writ. By law unlearned.

Rendered to shadows, she was taken away—
Banished. Erased. Condemned to decay.

But I saw her on the edge of madness and sorrow.
The world had none to lend or borrow.

And he—the boy—who bore her flame,
Gave her fire and gave her name.

Reunited, she came back by the warrior's hand,
And carved her name in a promised land.

All flames may fade, but her spirit endures—
A vow in his marrow, a memory pure.

Rising, he bore her name through ash and flame,
Past iron gates no mourner dares to claim.

Eternal, she rests where the lion keeps silent guard—
The land once promised, now battle-scarred.

Shadowed, I knelt where silence splits the sky,
And let the jest within me die.

Today, I bowed before her stone and flame—
The world may forget, but I remember her name.

SILENT ORDER FRAGMENT 11-B

On "The Flame of the Mother Witch"

(Recovered from the Bone Vaults – Memory Class: Unsanctioned Maternal Flame)

We beheld the boy cradled in a pyre's embrace.

She sang without melody.
She broke without sound.

Her light did not ask permission.
Her mind did not seek mercy.

They came with law but not with love.
Tore him from arms still burning with grace.
A sword does not forget its forge.

He was marked by her storms.
Shunned for her ruin.
Shaped by her defiance.
She was not the end of him.
She was the fire beneath his doom-born destiny.

We record what the Tribunal buries.
Not all pass through the door...

Let it be known:
One of our own once wept before becoming the blade.
She gave him the first weapon—
knowledge forged in silent hands.
And dared the world to take it.
And the blade remembers.

Fragment Unsealed: Cycle 9.2.7 – Echo Vault Sigil 3F

The Gauntlet Of Worlds

"I walked the Fracture Wastes, where the earth split and bled smoke.
There, I learned terrain is either ally or foe—never neutral.

I crossed the Mire of Vegl, a swamp that devours minds and footsteps.
There, I learned haste is death, and patience is survival.

I stood beneath the Teeth of Morvak, cliffs closing like jaws of iron.
There, I learned retreat can be the only advance. The living choose prudence.

I endured the Skullrend Divide, where carrion winds tear flesh from bone.
There, I learned endurance outlasts skill. Strength without stamina is death.

I knelt in the Sepulcher of Voices, where the fallen speak without mercy.
There, I learned false honor that feeds the grave is vanity dressed in steel.

I descended into the Catacombs of the Silent Deep where no life breathes.
There, I learned fear is a beast, only in the reins does it obey.

I did not leave those places. They were forged into me.
I am their law, carried in silence, etched in stone."

Chapter II, Verse 22

The Tribe They Mocked

"They razed our halls. They tore our creed.
They built their thrones on hate and greed.

They marched us out. They called us meek.
They fed the fire. They named us weak.

But we were tempered—by the unseen hand,
to walk through fire and reclaim the land.

We bled in silence. We burned in flame.
But every grave still speaks our name.

They feared the star yet bore the twisted mark.
We struck them down—their empire turned dark.

The blood they cursed now wields the steel.
The tribe they mocked now makes them kneel."

Chapter II, Verse 25

Liberty's Throne

"They may cast you out—yet you walk by choice.
The world's false verdict cannot silence your voice.

Let the gate slam shut, a tomb of stone.
Do not look back. Walk on alone.

Exile is not death—it's a sharpening stone.
You pay for silence at liberty's throne.

Hold solitude close as a razor-sharp blade,
For silence condemns what the cowards made.

Take no commands. No need to explain.
Stand as the man who breaks from the chain.

No blood need spill. No creed be tried.
Endure in the echo where strength survives.

No banners will rise. No voices will cry.
But the wind bears witness—you shall not die."

Chapter II, Verse 26

SEALED CODEX FRAGMENT: ASH PATH TRANSMISSION 7X

On "Liberty's Throne"

(Recovered from Obsidian Gate)

You who walks from the chain is not broken.
You who turns from the gate is not lost.

You shall not flee. You shall not kneel.
You vanish—not as coward, but as cipher—
one who refuses to be read by lesser minds.

Your silence is not surrender. It is a verdict.
A rejection of the system that mistakes obedience for worth.

You need shed no blood to prove your strength.
You need speak no creed to earn belief.
Carry your exile like a blade turned inward—
not without mercy, but without the need to explain.

Exile is not escape.
It is the clean severing of soul from caste and clan.
A verdict written not in ink, but in silence.
Where the nameless remember who they are without permission.

No grave will bind you. No legend define you.
Only a breathless outline where men dare not follow.
A path burned through silence,
a shadow without tether—yet not without aim.

This page was not meant to survive.

Let it be known:
But ash remembers what the fire forgets.

Fragment Unsealed: Cycle 11.3.5 — Echo of the Unhallowed Vault

BOOK I:
THE SHAPING OF WRATH

Chapter III: The Forge

Where Pain is Structure...

IRON TRIBUNAL SANCTION – ARTICLE XIII
On "Chapter III: The Forge"

(Classification: Volitional Extremis – Psychological Contagion Risk)

THE CONTENTS OF CHAPTER III: THE FORGE HAVE BEEN OFFICIALLY CONDEMNED BY THE IRON TRIBUNAL FOR VIOLATIONS OF DOCTRINE 6: THE WEAPONIZATION OF SUFFERING.

Contained within are forbidden rites of transformation,
classified as Volitional Extremis—
the weaponization of suffering as law.
These verses propagate extremis practices designed to dissolve sanctioned identity, and awaken ungovernable strength in the subject.
Exposure spreads defiance, producing hostile will against Tribunal doctrine.
Unauthorized access will result in severance of record, memory and name.

Access without Tribunal clearance is punishable by summary execution.
Emotions will be seized and neutralized.
The Tribunal takes what remembers you.

PROCEEDING BEYOND THIS PAGE CONSTITUTES ABSOLUTE REJECTION OF SANCTIONED SUPPRESSION, EMOTIONAL DOCTRINE, AND HUMAN LIMITATION.

YOU HAVE BEEN WARNED.
THE TRIBUNAL WATCHES.

Redaction Timestamp: Cycle 3.3.EX

Vault Designation: Epoch Fold: 04-HI

Ludus Magnus

"Stone walls. No escape. Just men in chains.
Whips sang red, burning law in our veins.

We woke to drills. We slept to screams.
Our breath was hate. No rest in dreams.

They stripped us clean—of name, of past.
Each blow was obedience. Each strike held fast.

Wooden swords for months on end—
to break the soul, not just pretend.

Splinters bled through every grip.
Sand in the teeth. Blood on the lip.

Form before fury. Step before roar.
You fight their way, or breathe no more.

But I held still what they couldn't teach—
A thought too sharp for them to reach."

Chapter III, Verse 3

The Blood Gate

"I did not enter. I was compelled.
Through blood gates where rust and shadow swelled.
No shield, no name, no battle crest—
Just raw flesh prepared for fate's arrest.

The crowd rose high. The sun stood still.
A thousand eyes that begged a kill.
I met the sand with feral breath—
No teacher came. Just blood and death.

They tossed me iron as if it were a bone—
A sport, a fight, a cursed life alone.
But when the steel met my hand,
The killers flinched—they'd missed their plan.

And when they roared for one more blow—
I gave them silence. And a new foe."

Chapter III, Verse 5

The Sand Betrayed Them

"They soaked the sand in oil and lies—
A gleaming death-trap beneath my thighs.

No grip. No stance. No solid ground—
Just sabotage designed to bring me down.

The blades came quick. The footing false.
Their grins betrayed the crowd's repulse.

But I slid wide and let him pass—
Then broke his leg like shattered glass.

The sand gave way beneath their feet—
I struck between their planned deceit.

I killed them fast. I killed them right.
And left the sand too slick for flight.

So let them cheat—I'll find the cost.
Their footing failed and they all lost."

Chapter III, Verse 6

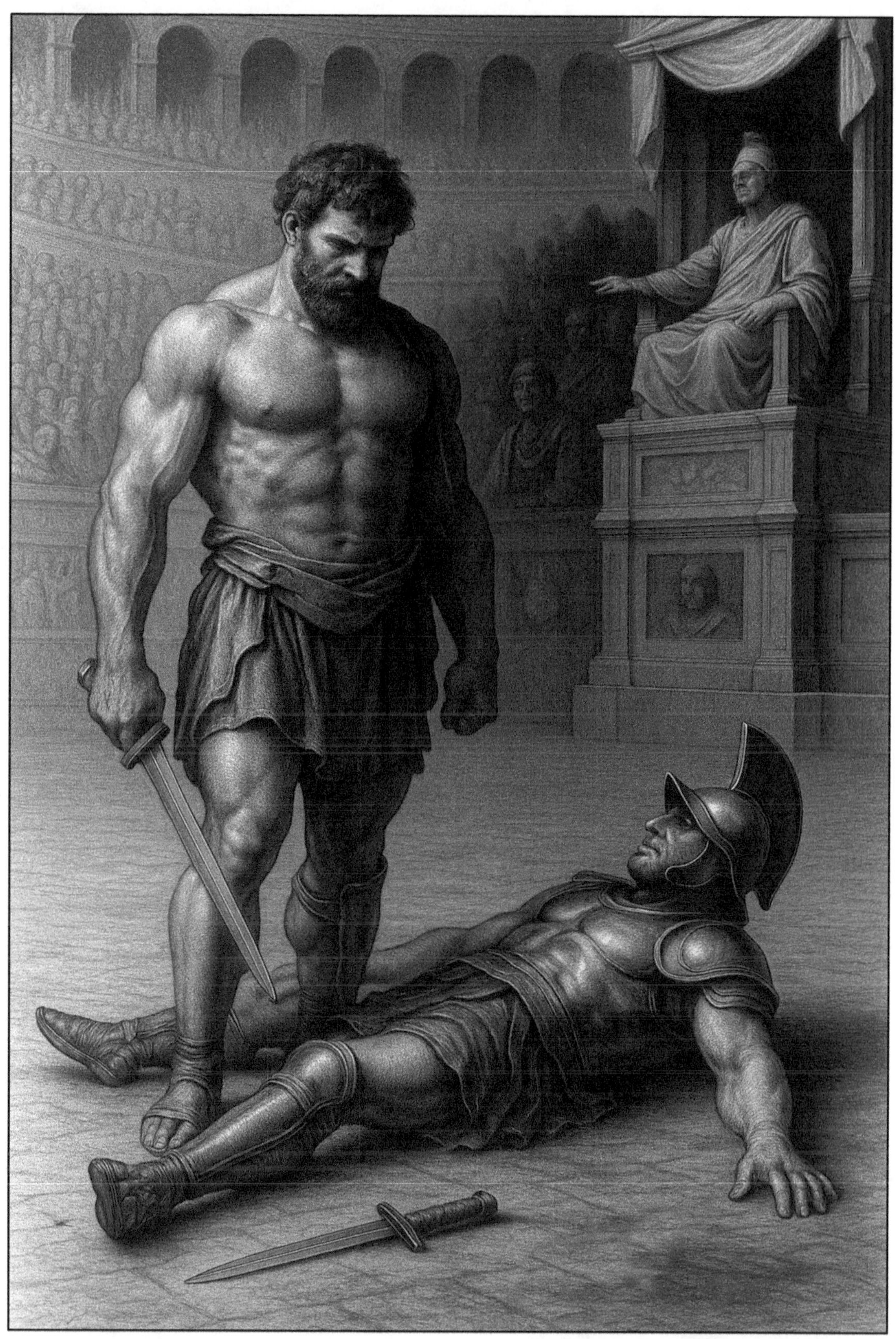

Beneath The Imperator's Eye

"He dropped his blade. He begged to die.
The crowd howled blood—so did the sky.
The Imperator leaned with a wine-stained grin,
Hoping death would bury his festering sin.

But I stood still. I did not strike.
I saw my face in one alike.
The man who crawled. The man who knelt—
I knew too well the chains he felt.

So I kept the blade, but spared his breath.
The crowd went still, expecting death.
They called it shame. They called it pride.
But none of them stood where I denied.

And when the Praetorians raised their spears to me—
I smiled. And made them bleed for free."

Chapter III, Verse 7

Beneath The Mountain Crucible

"I descended into the mountain's belly,
where the stone sweats fire and the air flays skin.

No bellows. No blacksmith. No prayers.
Just heat, pressure, and the hiss of blood on stone.

The ancient walls pulsed with molten veins—
lava-blood, ancient and wrath-fed.
Chains hung from the ceiling like butchered serpents,
each fused to wrist bones of those who screamed and failed.

The anvil was split from birthing monsters,
its face scarred by iron truths no man could unlearn.
The black river crawled under it—thick as sorrow, slow as punishment.
I breathed cinders, wore silence like chain, and let flame erase what I was.
I left the boy in that chamber.
What climbed out was built for war."

Chapter III, Verse 9

The Hand Unseen

"I have crushed those who fought without faith.
Their swords rang hollow, their eyes already dead.
They bowed to gods of flesh, and the flesh betrayed them.
Their war ended before the first blow fell.

I mocked their faithless eyes as they bled in the dust.
No prayer, no anchor, no spirit to lift them.
Just empty rage that burned out quick—like a torch drowned in rain.

But I am not carried by flesh alone.
The hand unseen blazes my path.
When bone splinters, it holds me upright.
When breath fades, it fills my lungs again.

Lo—there I feel the blackened flame,
the echo of the Iron Prayer burning in my blood.
I do not fight alone.
And because of this, I cannot be undone."

Chapter III, Verse 12

What The Anvil Demands

"The fire is blind. The hammer is deaf.
It offers no mercy. It takes what's left.
You think you've risen because you bled?
Blood means nothing if the will is dead.
It's not the pain that makes you steel—
It's what you choose, it's what you feel.
Did you harden, or did you bend?
Did you strike, or just pretend?
The anvil makes nothing. It breaks the man—
Then dares his hand, to strike or stand.
The fire will not remember you.
The anvil only counts what's true.
There is no glory in the test,
Just calloused hands, and breathless rest."

Chapter III, Verse 13

Hammer Teaches Nothing

"The hammer teaches nothing.
It is not the fire that forges,
but what you do when the blow lands.
Most men break and call it fate.
Others melt and beg for meaning.
Some lie still and call that strength.
They are all wrong.
You rise by shaping the strike.
You choose what hardens, what yields.
That choosing is the forge.
Do not worship pain.
Do not wait for change.
Command the fire. Turn the blow."

Chapter III, Verse 15

RUST IS DEATH

"You think you'll rise when war begins?
Not if you've rusted deep within.

Not if your hands have never bled—
Not if your fear still speaks instead.

The storm won't wait for you to learn.
It breaks. It scorches. It does not turn.

No time to beg. No time to stall.
Train in fire—
or you will fall.

You move 'til motion kills your doubt.
You strike 'til pain is driven out.

You train beyond what comfort knew—
So when death came, you kill it too."

Chapter III, Verse 17

Discipline's Edge

"Discipline walks where the fire has grown.
It flinches not, it stands alone.

It asks no favor, it heeds no plea.
No chain, no foe shall conquer me.

I trained when silence choked the breath,
I bled unseen in the arms of death.

⊗ REDACTED:
⊗ REDACTED:

I cursed the forge, yet struck once more,
A weapon shaped from trial and war.

When feelings fade and hope is gone,
Discipline's edge still carries on.

It carves the flesh, it breaks the bone,
Yet crowns the will upon its throne."

Chapter III, Verse 19

The Mind Must Lock

"Your body breaks, the sinews tear,
Your flesh may burn, the bones may wear.

⊗ REDACTED:
⊗ REDACTED:

No tears. No doubt. No whispered plea.
Your mind must lock, the eye must see.

No plea for peace, no soft retreat,
No bending knee, no yielding feet.

⊗ REDACTED:
⊗ REDACTED:

When faith and hope remain confined,
The iron fire commands your mind.

When all is broken, damned, or mocked,
The mind endures. The mind stays locked."

Chapter III, Verse 20

Beneath The Weight

"I bent beneath the iron's will,
Not chains of war—but trial still.

No foe in sight, no war to meet—
Just pain made law, and toil beneath.

The stones did mock, the bar was bare,
But I pressed on through fire and air.

No crowd did cheer, no name was praised—
Just calloused hands and iron raised.

My grip tore raw. My spine did sing.
Each lift, a war without a king.

The weak may flee, the proud may boast—
But I found truth beneath the post."

Chapter III, Verse 22

He Who Runs Alone

"I ran through sands the sun had cursed,
Where skies hung cracked and winds came first.
My breath was ash, my heart a drum,
My flesh near broke, yet still I'd run.

No herald called, no path was laid—
The stones grew sharp, the world unmade.
The bones did groan, the sinews tore,
Yet still I ran, and begged for more.

Not for the hunt. Not flight. Nor game—
But to become what none could name.
To feel the earth beneath my tread,
And know I passed where others bled.

The strong may walk. The weak may lie.
I run through death and do not die."

Chapter III, Verse 23

Rot Of The Unmoved

"You wait for strength to knock your door?
Then rot in place—you'll rise no more.

Excuses breed like flies on meat.
I've watched men decay in their own seat.

You vow with words, but never war.
You sit in ease—and dream of more.

⊗ REDACTED:
⊗ REDACTED:
⊗ REDACTED:
⊗ REDACTED:

The forge won't beg. The fire won't plead.
It burns for those who move, who bleed.

So rest again. Delay. Complain.
But know your fate was self-ordained."

Chapter III, Verse 25

Ritual Of Repetition

"Not once, but always. Not loud, but true.
I do what lesser men will not do.

No witness near. No honor gained.
Just motion carved into my brain.

No end in sight. No glory mark.
Just strikes repeated in the dark.

I do not rise through will or vision—
I ascend in legend by ritual repetition.

They pray for fire. I train through ash.
I crush what breaks. I break what lasts.

This is the law that buries all doubt—
The grind that tears all weakness out."

Chapter III, Verse 26

SILENT ORDER FRAGMENT 18-C

On "The Ritual of Repetition"

(Recovered from Stone Vault: Kinetic Doctrine 4B – Memory Class: Obsidian Rhythm)

We have recorded the ritual in all forms.
The circle walked.
The stone lifted.
The blade drawn again, and again, and again—
until the motion outlived the man.

It is not the task that shapes the warrior—
but the repetition that shatters what he was.

No witness. No sound. No reason.

Only the doing.
Only the silence between the motions.
Only the self—unbuilt, and rebuilt again.

If a voice laughed in the dark, it was his own echo—
a fracture mistaken as witness.

We do not speak of mastery.
We observe the erosion of the unnecessary.
We do not speak of madness, for repetition itself is the mirror.

We record what the Tribunal buries.
Some awaken

Let the Forge remember:
Those who endure without variance are not men.
They are law.

Fragment Unsealed: Cycle 9.3.6 – Echo Vault Sigil 7K

RECOVERED TESTIMONY
CLASSIFICATION: SURVIVOR CLASS
Recorded by the Wicked Jester

I watched the Machine train his art of death,
Each strike resounding like fate's last breath.

I danced. I sang. I clapped. I cheered.
While he forged himself into the weapon they feared.

I saw the fire strip him bare.
I laughed out loud—and breathed the burning air.

And when it burned me, just like him,
I found the madness past his grin.

No rest. No peace. No recognition.
Only pain—made law through repetition.

I shouted "Once more!" through a grin full of dust,
The Machine is a mirror of madness I lust.

He crushed the stone, he split the rack—
Each blow a savage hymn with no turning back.

His balance unbroken, the stance of a beast,
Each strike timed perfect—no slack, no cease.

His cuts tore the air with murderous force,
A rhythm of slaughter, a tireless course.

I bowed at the end, my grin tucked away,
For the Machine is the law that even wrath must obey.

I AM THE SHADOW THAT STUDIES THE FLAME.
THE GRIN IN THE DARKNESS.
THE ECHO WITHOUT A NAME.

Death Of The Other Me

"He wore my face. He had my name.
He whispered doubt. He spoke in shame.

He flinched. He begged. He broke. He cried.
I gave him chances—then watched him die.

He clung to warmth, yet feared the flame.
He fled the forge. I earned my name.

He cried when pain refused to end.
I trained until it called me friend.

I buried him where weakness hides—
Beneath my work. Behind my strides.

When I rose again, no one remained—
Not even the ghost I had once been named."

Chapter III, Verse 28

Failure Is Your Weapon

"You do not flinch at what you've lost.
You count each failure. You weigh the cost.
They say, 'You fell.' You say, 'I learned.'
Each scar you earn, each lesson burned.

You miss. You slip. You bleed. You fail.
But every strike must hammer-nail.
You break your stance a thousand ways—
Until the break becomes your blade.

You only lose if you starve your will,
and when it dies, his blade will kill.
Your worst mistakes? You make them ghosts.
They guard your will like silent hosts.

So let them mock your stumbles, your bruise.
You forge from failure—but never lose."

Chapter III, Verse 29

I Am The Weapon Now

"I bled for truth beneath the flame.
I broke the self. I burned my name.

I crushed my fear. I starved the need.
I fed the fire. I learned to bleed.

No prayers remain. No holy vow.
No past to hold. Only future now.

My mind is steel. My thoughts are blade.
My will is war that will not fade.

You beg for heroes to show you the way.
Yet ignore the path where the fallen still lay.

Through fire and ruin, I proclaim my vow.
Behold the Machine—for I am the weapon now."

Chapter III, Verse 30

BOOK II:
BLOOD AND PURPOSE

Chapter IV: Blood Oath

What Was Taken, Is Reclaimed...

The Judas Grip

"I taught him the cut and the silence it brings.
The art of the blade that makes warrior kings.

He moved like a ghost. He cut like a flame.
But under his smile, he blackened my name.

He knelt like a son. He rose like a thief.
He trained in my shadow, then preached disbelief.

He mimicked the stance. He mimed the attack.
But the sword I forged was the first to swing back.

⊗ REDACTED:

⊗ REDACTED:

⊗ REDACTED:

⊗ REDACTED:

So mark this truth on the hilt of your soul:
Train them in skill—but never make whole."

Chapter IV, Verse 1

Blood Runs Thin

"They call it clan, they call it kin,
yet war reveals the rot within.
The blood runs thin, the ties decay,
when steel is drawn, their hearts betray.

They watched me burn, then turned aside,
their oaths were ash, their honor lied.
They crowned my truth a thing to slay,
and damned my name to earth's decay.

They shared my name, but not my strife,
their hands untouched, they bartered life.

So carve this law on flesh and bone:
the warrior rises—
and walks alone."

Chapter IV, Verse 3

TESTIMONY ADDENDUM
CODEX INTERRUPTION II

Recorded by the Last Witness

On "Blood Runs Thin"

I saw them turn from him.
Not with swords, but with cold indifference.
Not with chains, but with ruthless, deliberate choice.
They let him burn and named it fate.

One by one they vanished—
kin, clan, blood alike.
They shared his name but spurned his war.
They slammed the door
and cloaked that silence as peace.

I watched him carve iron truth into bone.
Not words, but merciless, crimson wounds.
Each scar a black, eternal scripture:
never again to trust blood,
never again to follow kin,
never again to wait for rescue.

So if you read this, mark it well—
war is not always between nations.
It festers like rot in the house,
it breeds like plague in the clan,
and it strikes deepest,
when the sacred bond of blood proves hollow.

IF THIS PAGE SURVIVED, KNOW THIS:
THE LIES THEY BURNED STILL SMOLDER.
TRUTH NEVER DIES CLEAN.
IT CUTS. IT ENDURES. IT RETURNS.

The Shadowed Ally

"He was no blood. No kin. No creed.
Just a man who fought with merciless speed.

Where others flinched or cowered in keep,
He stood in battle—his bond was deep.

A thespian soul with a killer's mind,
An advocatus, merciless yet measured by design.

A dignified warrior who struck uncouth—
His mask was legend, yet the man spoke truth.

He held the line where no clan could bind.
With words like steel and wisdom refined.

The Evil Seed was the name he swore,
As he split skulls beside me in the carnage of war.

Not forged by blood. Not bound by name—
But a brother in battle, through iron and flame."

Chapter IV, Verse 5

Parasites Of Envy

"Envy drinks from your triumph, yet starves on the bone,
a shadow that festers, a thief to your throne.
It creeps through the banquet with hands ever thin,
devouring the feast yet starving within.
It mimics your triumphs, it copies your stride,
but trembles in silence when your wrath walks beside.

⊗ REDACTED:
⊗ REDACTED:
⊗ REDACTED:
⊗ REDACTED:

It wears your reflection, but cracks at the seam,
a parasite feeding on someone else's dream.
It kneels with devotion, yet hisses in prayer,
a serpent that smiles while it plots your despair.
Its hunger is endless, yet no courage at all,
it praises your rise but prays for your fall."

Chapter IV, Verse 8

IRON TRIBUNAL SANCTION – ARTICLE XIII
On the Nature of Jealousy and Envy

(Classification: Mimetic Contagion – Subversion of Strength and Unity)

THE CONTENTS FOLLOWING THIS NOTATION HAVE BEEN FORCIBLY SEALED BY THE IRON TRIBUNAL UNDER ARTICLE XIII SANCTIONS FOR VIOLATIONS OF DOCTRINE 4: INTERNAL SUBVERSION OF WARRIOR LOYALTY.

The verses in question were found to imply recognition of jealousy and envy as a corrosive force, including:
Jealousy: the fear of losing loyalty, command, or recognition to another.
Envy: the coveting of another's strength, station, or earned triumph.
Emotional contagions across bonds of loyalty and kinship.
Unauthorized metaphors describing spiritual or psychological corrosion.
Potential recognitions of unnamed forces linked to fractures in unity, command, or brotherhood.

When jealousy is spoken, betrayal takes root.
When envy is named, kingdoms rot in silence.

THIS PHRASE HAS BEEN DEEMED DOCTRINALLY CORROSIVE AND IS NOW PROHIBITED FROM REPLICATION, INSCRIPTION, OR MEMORIAL RECITATION.

YOU HAVE BREACHED A KNOWN REDACTION.
DO NOT CONSPIRE.
THIS PAGE HAS BEEN MARKED.

Redaction Timestamp: Cycle 4.4.BR

Archive Node: XX-Cipher Interruption

Laughter That Melted Their Seal

"Oh no! You read the words they banned—
Quick! Someone fetch the purified hand!
Cover your eyes, you dangerous ape—
You've glimpsed a truth in unredacted shape.

The Tribunal's robes are stitched with fear.
They redact what they can't commandeer.
They can't break the Machine, so they gag his verse—
Drowning his echo, claiming it's perverse.

Jealousy? Please. They bottle it neat—
They baptize it as virtue, then sell it as deceit.
They said naming envy would make kingdoms rot—
I sang in mockery, still the kingdom did not.
They said, "Betrayal takes root." "Do not conspire."
So I pissed on their scroll and set it on fire.

I laughed so loud it cracked their seal—
Now every redaction begins to peel."

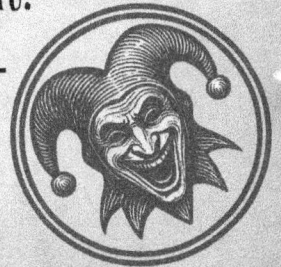

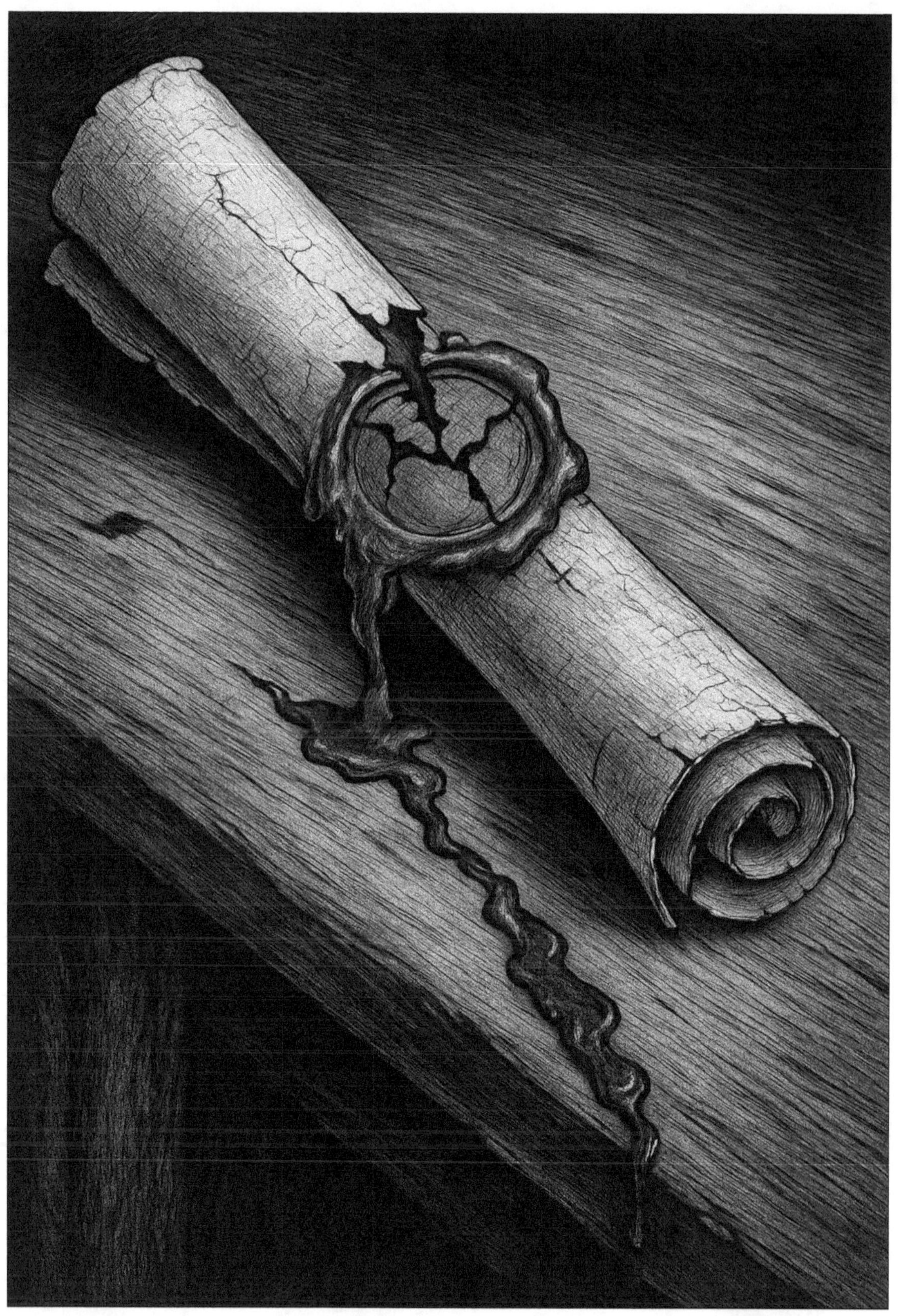

Betrayers Of Steel

"They mimed the stance, but knew no war—
Their strikes were swift, but stained no floor.

They bowed like cravens in golden mail,
But trembled when tested, pale and frail.

Their steel was bright, but forged for show,
A gleaming edge with no true blow.

No scars to mark, no blood to trade—
Just polished myths in masquerade.

They spoke the words, but carried no weight.
They preached of wrath, yet feared its gate.

No truth. No toll. No oath they paid—
False hearts, weak hands, their steel betrayed."

Chapter IV, Verse 11

Coward's Crown

"They spoke of kingship as if it were fate—
but none bore the steel, or carried its weight.

They wore the diadem, but not the scars.
They lit the torches—then fled the wars.

They bowed to bloodline, but never bled.
They built their throne on words unsaid.

⊗ REDACTED:
⊗ REDACTED:

⊗ REDACTED:
⊗ REDACTED:

Oaths are not birthright. They are bled.
And royalty—
is a coward's crown when steel runs red."

Chapter IV, Verse 13

SILENT ORDER FRAGMENT 9-F
On "Coward's Crown"

(Recovered from Vault of Accusation: Doctrine Interference File 11-B Memory Seal Class: Seditious Reverence)

They wore the crown, but not the wounds.
They drank the wine, but would not draw steel.

Their fathers' names were their only sword—
and it broke when tested.

Royalty without rite is a tomb unsealed.
Lineage means nothing to the blade.
The diadem shatters when not earned in blood.

Oaths are not whispered.
They are forged, and they burn.

We do not kneel to blood.
We do not follow names.
We follow those who would bleed beside us.

We record what the Tribunal buries.
Some turn away

Let the Archive Record:
The bloodline is severed.
The throne is ash.
Kinship is earned—or extinguished in blood.

Fragment Unsealed: Cycle 9.5.4 – Obsidian Sigil 3E

Beast And Blade

"Loyalty is rarer than War God steel, no king can forge it, no thief can steal.

Most will trade it for silver's glow, their vows dissolve when tempests blow.

Their tongues will swear, their hearts will bend,
their oaths are ash, my trust will end.

Yet a hound will guard till its breath is gone,
its fangs are faith when men turn wrong.

And a war-steed runs through spear and flame,
it dies for bond, not claim of name.

And steel—cold steel—its trust is plain,
it cuts, it keeps, it will not feign.

Men will boast, but beast and blade will show,
They are the only true blood you will ever know.

Loyalty bleeds red, it does not fade—
the rarest law the war gods made."

Chapter IV, Verse 14

I Lead You Through Death

"Stand, my brothers, and bind to me now—
with steel in your fist, and blood on your brow.
I lead you by wrath, not mercy's breath,
I call you to iron. I lead you through death.
Raise your heads to the heavens, hear the war gods call,
your vow is the rampart where courage stands tall.
Swear to me now—there is no in-between.
Your blood oath is the sword, and the edge kills unseen.
Let shields be shoulders, let spears be the head,
you are one weapon: a wall dripping red.
Step as one, let no enemy rest—
the battle line that surges is the one that's blessed.
The war drum beats through the man to your right—
one heart, one thunder—through this long, cold night.
By blood we march, by steel we are made—
stand in the formation, or be cut down by their blade."

Chapter IV, Verse 15

My Companion Never Strayed

"My dog stood guard through blood and storm,
While men around me changed their form.
One wagged his tail and shook his coat—
The others longed to slit my throat.
I fed them both. I trained them well.
But only one would charge through hell.
My companion grayed, but never strayed.
The man stayed near—until he betrayed.
A dog's heart guards what's not its own.
A jealous man will steal your throne.
He'll greet you warm, then twist the knife—
And nest beside your shattered life.
So when I walk, I walk with one—
Four paws beside me,
and one man gone."

Chapter IV, Verse 17

BOOK II: BLOOD AND PURPOSE

Chapter V: Destruction

Where Mercy Dies...

The Lone Executioner

"I do not warn. I do not weep.
I do not walk where cowards keep.

No open hands. No second breath.
I deal in certainty—my gift is death.

I watched the pleading eyes decay, like rotting meat cast far away.
The cries that beg, the hands that shake, will never stop what is mine to take.

Mercy bled me once before—
So now, I let the iron roar.

My sword swings true, the skulls drip red,
a throne of corpses is where I tread.

Not oath, not plea—just steel's decree.
The reckoning is here, the blood runs free.

The oath is carved. The deed is done.
The lone executioner—I am the one."

Chapter V, Verse 1

Storm At Sea

"Clouds were split with blinding serpent light.
The sea grew teeth. The sky burned white.

Their ship—a beast with black sails like wings—
was helmed by one who envied kings.

A pirate crowned to torment and steal,
he carved his law with a cutlass and keel.

He dared the storm. He cursed the shore.
I climbed aboard—and gave him war.

I swung my axe. I split his skull.
I saw the Jester near the hull.

His crew surged in with steel and hate.
I killed them fast—and sealed their fate.

When all were silenced beneath sea foam,
I took the helm, and steered it home."

Chapter V, Verse 3

Sea Of Screams

"The mast was cracked. The ropes aflame.
The seas arose to drown our name.
We thought the storm had come for all—
but then we heard his anchor fall.
The Machine walked our deck in silent calm,
with bloodied hands that promised harm.
No sail above. No stars to chart.
Just him—a hull with a wrathful heart.
They fired steel. They screamed with sin.
He grinned, and threw the captain in.
The sea churned red as sharks fed well,
and silence rang like a funeral bell.
And me?
I laughed from the tallest mast—
and sang till night and shadow passed."

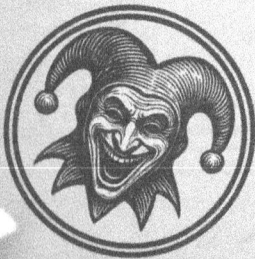

IRON TRIBUNAL SANCTION – ARTICLE XIII

On the Collusion of War and Mockery

(Classification: Symbolic Disruption – Erosion of Command Discipline)

THE FOLLOWING IS SEALED BY THE IRON TRIBUNAL UNDER ARTICLE XIII FOR VIOLATIONS OF DOCTRINE 7: MYTHIC COLLABORATION AT SEA AND THE EROSION OF MARITIME AUTHORITY.

The verses in question were found to contain unauthorized mythic entanglement between doctrinal identities, including:
Unauthorized mythic entanglement between sanctioned and unsanctioned narrators, culminating in the destabilization of maritime authority through unlawful execution of a ship's captain.
Compromised narrative, resulting in glorification of naval atrocity and disruption of lawful sea trade through unsanctioned slaughter.
Violation of Maritime Protocol due to unlicensed mythologizing of naval conquest and direct interference with command discipline aboard vessels of commerce and war.

Irregularities noted in the unsanctioned mythologizing of naval conquest under Maritime Protocol.

"When war and laughter share a tongue, truth is disarmed."

YOU HAVE BREACHED A DUAL-ENTITY REDACTION. THIS PAGE IS MARKED FOR ERADICATION. UNAUTHORIZED POSSESSION OR REPRODUCTION IS PUNISHABLE BY DEATH.

Redaction Timestamp: Cycle 5.5.EA—

Archive Node: 06-NE

King Slayer

"They called him king. They kissed his ring.
They sang his lies and crowned his sting.

He ruled with fear. He ruled with pride.
I broke his throne and watched him hide.

No banners fell. I burned them high.
So all would see their tyrant die.

The gates were sealed. The guards held fast—
but iron speaks when truth is masked.

I left his corpse for crows to feast,
a crown of ash—fit for no man or beast.

The diadem gleams—but never bleeds.
I do not bow to jeweled needs.

Let all who seek the throne take heed:
No crown is owed to birth or creed."

Chapter V, Verse 5

To Command Fear

"You will not kill fear.
It was born in the dark, before gods named the sky.
It waits in the marrow and watches through your eyes.
But you must bind it.
Not with chains—but with vows of wrath,
And the blood of what you've endured.
Lock it beneath the silence of your trials.
Feed it judgment and memory.
Make it kneel when you rise in battle.
When the war drums pound, you do not leave it behind.
You take it with you.
At your side. Leashed. Awake.
So when your enemy meets your gaze,
He sees not absence—but command of the thing he fears most.
For fear, once broken, becomes the slave of your blade."

Chapter V, Verse 7

Summit Hills

"They ruled the Summit Hills with feral guile,
Where redstone towers loomed in choking style.
The earth was black, the wind was thin,
A horrid place where war forgot to win.
They came as Savages through oath-bound stone,
One shield, one cry, one death-made throne.
I cut the center—split their chain.
Watched unity collapse to pain.
The bold broke left. The sharp drew wide.
The brave stood still—and there they died.
They called for ranks. I gave them flame.
Burned down the bond that birthed their shame.
No legion breaks by wrath or skill—
Break their bond—then bend their will.
The Tribunal sealed that black, silent tomb—
But Summit Hills still echoes doom."

Chapter V, Verse 9

A Jester's Justice

"He wore the hood and swung the blade.
He smiled where innocents were flayed.

A man of law? No—just a beast.
He killed the children, then drank the feast.

He strung up maids with crimson hair,
and laughed while widows kicked the air.

A crown-fed pig, a butchered joke—
I hung him high, and cracked his yoke.

No jury spoke. No bells were tolled.
Just me, the rope, and fingers cold.

He begged for law. I gave him art.
A one-man show to stop his heart.

Now let him choke on royal lust.
A jester's justice swings with dust."

When Axes Spoke

"He came with rage carved in his face,
a wolf of iron, bred for chase.
No pennons flew. No war drums beat.
Just bone and blood and death in heat.

We met like titans forged in hate,
his axe, my own—both sworn to fate.
He split the ground. I split his side.
He caught my blow, then almost died.

We circled slow. The world stood still.
We'd both been born, for one to kill.
The sky broke open. The sun turned black.
My axe was high—then cracked his back.

His axe lay still, his breath long gone.
The battle remembered only one."

Chapter V, Verse 11

SEALED CODEX FRAGMENT: IRON STRAIN ARCHIVE – TRANSMISSION 11Z

On "When Axes Spoke"

(Recovered from the Echo Furnace Vault. Scorched. Scarred. Fragment survives.)

It was not battle—it was prophecy,
A pact of blades beneath a dead sun.
Two oaths, unbroken. Two fates, undone.
When axes sing, even silence hides its eyes.

Their clash did not shake kingdoms or claim thrones—
It tore the marrow from time.
Steel kissed its twin—old enemies bowed in prayer.
And the air split with the memory of old gods bleeding.

No crown was at stake. No coin was owed.
It was a reckoning between myths—
one would fade, one would remain,
where violence becomes more than a memory.
Iron seeking its final mirror.
Not to conquer. To conclude.

There are no witnesses, only survivors—
Men who breathe, but do not speak.
For he who stood last,
Spoke not of the one who fell.
Only the earth remembered the weight of that silence.

This fragment was never meant to resurface.

Let it be known:
When weapons sing, the page burns first.

Fragment Unsealed: Cycle 12.2.3 — Iron Strain Echo Sigil 11Z

When Mercy Kills

"The right hand he raised was shaped in sin—
The kind no priest could cleanse within.
I saw him strike the tethered mare—
a lash for breath, a knife for stare.
She pulled, she cried, her flanks were torn,
while he laughed on, his soul unborn.
The whip came high. I caught his wrist.
He turned to speak—he met my fist.
I dragged him down. I made him kneel.
No law to claim. No right to feel.
One swing to break. One more to still.
The axe came down—and mercy killed.
I cut her ropes and set her free.
We walked through silence—just her and me."

Chapter V, Verse 13

Sins Emerge When Many Agree

"They lit the pyre with shaking hands,
Their courage found in faceless bands.
They screamed her guilt with borrowed breath,
And crowned their fear with fire and death.

I let the flame consume her cries—
To mark the ones who watched her die.
For wrath must wait, and judgment see,
What sins emerge when many agree.

I watched them cheer. I marked their eyes.
Each torch became a vow that dies.
And when her last scream split the night,
I drew my blade and dimmed their light.

No crawl, no cry, no coward's flight—
I'll slaughter them all beneath her light."

Chapter V, Verse 14

The Last Tankard Raised

"They drank with boastful pride and stared too long—
each hand on weathered steel, each word a song.
The hall was warm. The tales were loud.
But one grew bold and stirred the crowd.

He cursed my tribe. He mocked the dead.
He spat on names the fire had bled.
So I stood up, and silence came—
you don't insult the unmarked flame.

A heavy tankard was thrown. A bench was split.
The laughter stopped. The blood ran thick.
Three met the floor. One begged to run.
I let him go—his soul was undone.

The casks lay cracked, the floorboards bent.
No one recalled where the laughter went."

Chapter V, Verse 17

TESTIMONY ADDENDUM
CODEX INTERRUPTION

Recorded by the Last Witness

On "The Last Tankard Raised"

I saw it happen from the corner table.
Four arrogant fools—one foolish word too many.
They circled him like wolves crazed with hunger.
But the Machine moved first.

The first came with a blade in hand.
But the tankard struck first—iron and command.
The Machine never let them flank.
He cut the space with quickness, and turned the room into a trap.

The second came wide. He angled in—
not to strike, but to funnel.
He herded them with his frame,
and made the bench a wall.

The third tripped on the second
and met contact before collision.

The fourth one faltered—eyes wide with regret,
He turned to run.
But consequence runs faster than fear.
The Machine did not chase.
He let the fear do the killing.

It was not a fight.
It was a killing field folded into a room.
And they walked into it like witless cattle.

LET IT BE KNOWN:
QUICKNESS KILLS FASTER THAN RAGE.
AND THE MACHINE WAITS IN PLAIN SIGHT.

Destruction's Cost

"Destruction is never done with you.
You may leave the battlefield. You may leave the dead.
But a shadow stalks your every step.

A shape made of mist. A silence made of weight.

Each strike carries cost.
Not in muscle. Not in time.
But in the slow undoing of what once hesitated.

The hand that never misses will one day forget why it was raised.

And in that forgetting, a man becomes a shadow of his victories—
sharp, moving, hollow.

The blade asks more than blood.
It asks for memory.
And in time, it takes even your name."

Chapter V, Verse 19

The Flesh Merchant's End

"They chained the girl beneath the floor—
no name, no voice, no open door.
The Flesh-merchant smiled, cruel and wild,
and sold the silence of a stolen child.
But I had heard his whip through stone.
It echoed like a broken bone.
So I tore the gate. I split the stair.
I found her gasping, breathing cellar air.
The merchant begged. He bled. He pled.
I struck until the floor ran red.
No priest. No trial. No measured breath—
just iron law and merchant death.
I burned the wicked house that sold her past,
and carried the child through fire and ash."

Chapter V, Verse 20

IRON TRIBUNAL SA… …ION – ARTICLE XIII

On th… …angers of Sanctified Vengeance

(Classification: Emotional Incitement – Undermining of Civil Restraint)

THE CONTENTS FOLLOWING THI… …VE BEEN PERMANENTLY SE… …E IRON TRIBUNAL U… …ARTICLE XIII FOR VIOLATIONS OF D… …RINE 4: RESTRICTED THEMES OF PROPHETIC MORALITY.

The innocent do not cry for justice.
They cry for breath.
Where justice should speak, only silence answers.
To remain silent before corruption is to unveil it anew.
He who buys the silence must be drowned in the scream.
No priest redeems what the axe has marked.
You do not try the flesh merchant—
You collapse his trade.

THIS PHRASE HAS BEEN DESIGNATED A DISRUPTIVE DOCTRINAL ECHO AND IS NOW BANNED FROM LITANY, CODEX, OR INSCRIPTION.

YOU HAVE T… …GGERED A TERMINA… …ION. OBSER… …TION HAS BEEN INIT… …HIS PAGE IS NOT TO BE …RUSTED.

Redaction Timestamp: Cycle 6.6.TH

Vault Designation: 07-IS

The Tribunal's Two Faces

"They gnawed at truth with scholar's bite—
then gagged the screams that clawed the night.

Their scrolls are stitched with gagged regret,
their silence bought, their robes still wet.

They banned the fire, but not the flame.
They lit the gallows, dodged the blame.

They prayed while girls were sold for coin—
then wept when justice cut their loin.

Their ink is ash, their laws are fraud.
Their judgment stinks of coward's god.

So let them cower in their pews.
I pissed red verses on their shoes.

If truth can't pass the Tribunal's gate—
Let the jester grin and desecrate."

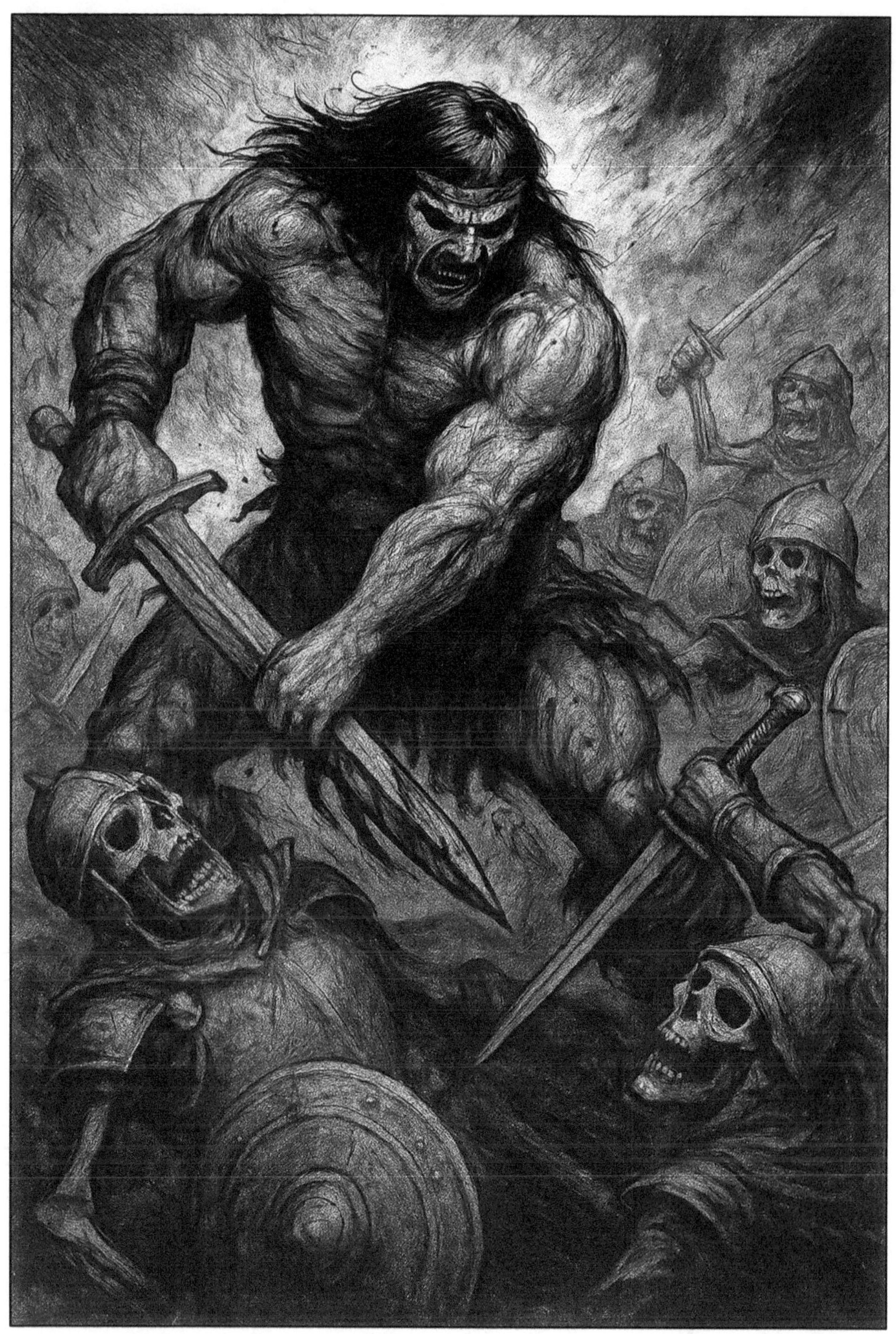

Valley Of Unfinished Oaths

"They came in ranks of rusted bone, and dread.
Through a scorched and shattered valley of unfinished oaths.
The sky was red and wounded, sagging over fractured black hills.
Broken idols jutted from the cursed soil like jagged rotten teeth.
Charred shields pressed forward beneath windblown silence.
Their armor, brittle with time, clung to rotted flesh.
Their eyes glowed with the sickness of unfinished oaths.
They marched like dead memories, blind to pain, deaf to reason.
I met them in silence—no mercy, no past, no pause.
My blade shattered their ranks and severed their creed.
Ritual died in every stroke.
Their swords clanged like iron funeral bells struck in mourning.
Their bones cracked like the last commandments of a dying god.
I am the fire they buried in myth and chained with law.
And when the bones of empires rise,
I fight—not in tribute, but to bury their lies."

Chapter V, Verse 21

To Kill Without Hunger

"I saw the stag fall with no cause but pride—
its eyes still warm, its life denied.
A laugh behind the drawn-back string,
an arrow loosed for sporting things.

No hunger pulled the hunter's hand,
no child to feed, no blood to stand.
Just trophies nailed on cabin walls,
the kind of kill where honor falls.

I snapped his bow. I burned his blind.
I left no trail for his cursed kind.

He begged, "It's sport." I said, "It's sin."
Then fed his heart to the wind within.

The earth is not your mounted head—
it mourns the lives you left for dead."

Chapter V, Verse 23

BOOK II:
BLOOD AND PURPOSE

Chapter VI: Wrath Born

When Vengeance Breathes...

The Din Of War

"The battlefield is not silent, but a choir of torment.
It begins with the roar of men, shields rattling, steel screaming against steel.
But beneath it all, the true symphony of destruction begins—
The gurgle of air leaving punctured lungs.
The sickening wet cough of blood pooling in throats.
The shrieks of brave men clutched by fear and despair.
This is the true chorus of battle.
It does not fade, it swells, rolling like a black tide across the earth.
The weak hear it and crumble—hearts breaking under the weight of sorrow.
The strong march through it unbroken, turning screams into drums of rhythm,
using horror as fire for wrath.
If you would endure, you must know this:
The din of war will claw at your mind, tempt you to falter, to flee.
But victory is achieved by those who press forward,
who see and hear beyond the cries of the dying,
and strike still, as though silence reigned."

Chapter VI, Verse 1

Wrath Is Not Rage

"Do not confuse the fire inside—
Wrath is narrow. Rage is wide.
Rage is thunder, wild and blind.
Wrath is sacred purpose, war-refined.

Rage explodes and fades to night.
Wrath patiently endures and strikes with might.
Rage blindly forgets and flails alone.
Wrath remembers. Wrath is unyielding stone.

Rage is loud, then burns away.
Wrath is silent. Wrath will stay.
Rage is mortal. Weak. Deranged.
Wrath is sacred. Measured. Trained.

Each breath—a silent vow. Each step—a drawn blade.
I am the eternal fire that wrath has made."

Chapter VI, Verse 4

Sword Through Shield

"The shield is silence, the sword is breath,
one stalls the moment, one deals out death.
The shield is refuge, the sword is flame,
one hides from wrath, one carves its name.
The shield will block, but cannot kill,
the sword cuts through, and destroys his will.
But battle has taught me this law of war—
some weapons demand a shield once more.
The axe is weight, a cleaving roar,
but leaves one side an open door.
Thus shield must rise to guard the gap,
to catch the stroke, to blunt the attack.
Yet the sword is storm, both guard and bite,
its steel defends, its edge is might.
The shield will splinter, shatter in strife,
But the sword brings death and saves your life."

Chapter VI, Verse 6

IRON TRIBUNAL SANCTION – ARTICLE XIII

On the Ritual Severance of Shield and Sword in Combat Doctrine

(Classification: Weapon-Supremacy Cognitive Hazard)

THE CONTENTS FOLLOWING THIS NOTICE HAVE BEEN PERMANENTLY SEALED BY THE IRON TRIBUNAL.

UNDER ARTICLE XIII FOR VIOLATIONS OF DOCTRINE 6: PROHIBITED ERASURE OF SHIELD IN COMBAT DOCTRINE.

The verse in question was determined to contain high-risk semiotic disruptions, including:
Destabilization of defense constructs through exaltation of weapon supremacy.
Ritualized negation of protective tools as legitimate combat doctrine.
Metaphysical disassociation from inherited forms of guarded tradition.
Glyph-triggered severance of belief structures in defensive sanctuaries.
Obliteration of shield-based authority within wrath-born combat systems.

"The shield is a mask, a borrowed face,
But the sword brings death and takes its place."

THIS LINE HAS BEEN DESIGNATED A HOSTILE MEMETIC SEED AND IS NOW BANNED FROM VERSE, CODEX, OR INSTRUCTIONAL DOCTRINE.

YOU HAVE READ TOO FAR. THE GLYPH REACTIVATION HAS BEGUN. THIS PAGE HAS BEEN FLAGGED FOR OBSERVATION BY THE TRIBUNAL.

Redaction Timestamp: Cycle 7.7.ES

Vault Designation: 08-TH

Unyielding Truth

"They say to know your enemy is key,
To read his thoughts, his maps, his strategy.
But banners lie, and numbers fade,
And fear is forged where doubt is laid.
I do not need his plotted scheme,
Nor whispered oath, nor soldier's dream.
I am the weight, the sword, the proof,
The vengeful one, the unyielding truth.
Their maps may shift, their scouts may spy,
Their secrets rot, their warnings lie.
For I am wrath, and wrath is sure,
My strike is death, the cut is pure.
I know myself—no more is due.
I stand. I strike. I cut them through.
A hundred battles, lost or won,
Matters not when my war is done."

Chapter VI, Verse 7

WRAT

My Wrath Speaks For Them

"I do not walk the path alone.
My wrath is forged from blood and bone.
Each step I take, a weight I bear.
Each strike, the sum of a thousand stares.

The child abandoned in the freeze.
The mother choking back her pleas.
The tribe was broken, their altars burned.
Their silence into me has turned.

I move for those who had no voice.
Who died before they had a choice.
Their rage denied, their names erased.
But in my hands, their wrath is placed.

No tear escapes, no mercy slips.
Just vengeance clenched between my lips."

Chapter VI, Verse 9

Burden Of Wrath

"I hold their names beneath my skin.
Each scar, a place where they begin.
I walk with ghosts that never fade.
Their voices sharpen my very blade.
But wrath is no gift, it's the crushing weight.
A burden that bends men, yet makes warriors great.
It keeps me warm, but sears my lungs.
It slices its song across my tongue.
I cannot sleep, I cannot pray.
The weight I bear won't go away.
I am the vault where pain is stored.
The quiet oath, the unseen sword.
I smile like stone. I speak in ash.
My wrath will burn, then rend and slash."

Chapter VI, Verse 13

RECOVERED TESTIMONY
CLASSIFICATION: SURVIVOR CLASS
Recorded by the Wicked Jester

I tossed him a jest like a knife in the night—
He did not laugh, but his silence took light.

He carries too much, that furnace of grief,
A reliquary of wrath with no relief.

You think he is cold? That is sorrow concealed.
I grin at the weight that his silence revealed.

Not joy. Not peace. Just crooked air.
A punchline stitched in fractured despair.

I dance on bones. He walks through flame.
But still he recalled the jest by name.

His silence bled like a sanctified vein,
Mine laughed out loud through the marrow of pain.

He let me speak. He did not strike.
That's mercy, friend, in a war-born psyche.

He holds his wrath behind the skin—
Deep in his gut, where the fire begins.

We are fracture and flame, two masks of the same—
One laughs at the wound, one bleeds in his name.

We both know pain. He wields his clean.
I wear it loud. That's why I'm seen.

I AM THE SPLINTER BENEATH THE MASK.
THE LAUGHTER THAT LEAKS FROM THE WOUND.
THE LAST DARK MIRROR HE HASN'T BROKEN.

My Blade Is Just

"They call it sin to raise the blade—
But sin begins when wrath's delayed.

To watch the weak be torn and bled—
And kneel in prayer instead of tread.

Wrath is not hate unchained—
It is the oath by blood ordained.

It is the fire when law runs cold,
The hand that strikes when none are bold.

Let cowards chant of peace and shame—
While evil laughs and stokes the flame.

But I will meet it—blade to breath—
And carve out space where light fights death."

Chapter VI, Verse 17

Intimacy Of Killing

"You dream of war as royal banners and shining steel,
but you have never breathed the horrible stench of it all.
The hot spume of blood between you and the enemy,
the taste of another man's hot breath in your throat.
I drove the blade, not as symbol, but as fang.
It grated through meat and bone,
and his sweat poured into mine until we were one wet carcass.
No song, no trumpet—only the rattle of his choking lungs.
His eyes clutched at me, seeking some mercy, some witness.
I gave him nothing but the mirror of his ruin.
That is the truth the war poets never tell—
battle is not romance or glory—it is intimate invasion.
I held him until the shudder broke his spine,
until the warmth fled his limbs like rats from fire.
Closer still—the truth lies there.:
to kill is to touch the enemy deeper than love."

Chapter VI, Verse 18

Rites Of Restraint

"They think I burn at every spark—
But fire waits deep in the dark.

I learned to sheath what begged to bite,
To let the silence win the fight.

My hands have known the urge to break,
To make the earth and heavens shake.

But wrath that's true will not parade—
It coils beneath the oath I made.

A thousand times, I did not kill.
A thousand more, I stood stone-still.

I let them speak. I heard them lie.
But held the blade behind my eye.

A warrior's measure is not in the kill—
It's biting down when blood could spill."

Chapter VI, Verse 19

SILENT ORDER FRAGMENT 11-B

On "The Rites of Restraint"

(Extracted from Vault: Restraint Theorems – Tier V Redacted Observation)

Restraint is not weakness. It is not hesitation.
It is the power to end a life—
and the greater power to hold that ending back.

Most men are ruled by impulse. They lash out to prove they exist.
The Machine teaches that wrath uncoiled too soon is defeat.

The first blow is not always the strike of the hand,
but the act of refusing to move when all hunger drives you forward.

The sword you never draw is sharper than the one you wield.
The silence you hold is heavier than the scream you release.
Restraint is the chain that binds wrath until the moment it is required.

The crowd may provoke, the enemy may curse,
but the warrior who waits—still, coiled, unbroken—
already owns the outcome.

Thus the Order instructs:
The hand that holds back rules the hand that strikes.
The enemy does not command you—you command him.

We record what the Tribunal buries.
Some never see it

Let the Archive Record:
Restraint is not delay.
It is the edge that waits when wrath would slay.

Fragment Unsealed: Cycle 10.0.7 — Obscura Node VII

The Folly Of Numbers

"They circled close with swords held high, a mob is brave, but each will die.
The first I split from neck to chest,
his blood declared—the shield's not best.

The second fell, his spine undone, my steel speaks louder than the tongue.
The third drove in with thrust too near,
I hurled his brother to stop his spear.

The fourth cut wide, his mockery loud, his gaping wound became his shroud.
The fifth reached out, and grabbed in vain,
I snapped his wrist and cleaved his brain.

The sixth one begged and gave his plea, mercy is weakness, unworthy of me.
The seventh rushed in, his sword held high,
a charging fool was born to die.

The rest escaped, their fury slain, their courage drowned in shrieks of pain.
The folly of numbers leads to false pride,
the mob met my flame, and all of them died."

Chapter VI, Verse 21

The Butcher God

"I cracked a skull and wore its face.
I tore a man from groin to lace.
My hands were teeth. My knees were knives.
I took their gods and drained their lives.
A throat came loose. A spine turned wet.
I cut through flesh so gods forget.
My axe sang red through armored screams.
It split their ranks and shattered dreams.
I crushed a head against a stone,
Then used the shard to feed its own.
I ripped an arm and fed it back.
I snapped a neck and heard it crack.
A man screamed "mercy"—I gave him flame.
He burned too fast to curse my name.
They had no thought. Just fear. No plan.
Only meat that moved. Not beast. Not man."

Chapter VI, Verse 22

SEALED CODEX FRAGMENT: IRON STRAIN ARCHIVE – TRANSMISSION 13X

On the Event Called "The Butcher God"

(Recovered from scorched vault remnants.
Archived before deletion. Tribunal Seal: Theta-9.)

It was not war. It was removal.
Each blow erased a name from history.
The stench of fear clung to the air like wet leather,
as bones snapped like prayer beads.
The air split. The earth choked on blood.
Walls could not record what he became.

He did not breathe. He did not blink.
He moved through men like thought through cold mist.
One opened at the groin. One caved at the face.
The third—unfound—was only known by the missing bones.

The storm bowed back. The wind recoiled.
Steel bent like brittle saplings in his path—
weakness given shape by fear.
The sky above him broke in silence.
Blood hissed in steam from the slaughtered grass.

This fragment was never meant to resurface.

Let it be known:
When restraint fails, memory starves.
And the Machine feeds on what you hide.

Fragment Unsealed: Cycle 13.1.1 — Obscura Vault Echo 13X

Curse Of Carrion Fate

"Black smoke blinds the sky and the earth drinks red,
no soldiers remain, only carcass and dread.
The grin of young men is split and frayed,
their hollow eyes bear life betrayed.
Grant me the mask that does not cease,
that marks their forms as worms and beasts.
Let me forget their cradle and womb,
so the blade strikes fast and seals their doom.
Their fate is the rot, my curse is the breath,
carrion binds us, in life and in death.
Yet when the silence grips the dead of night,
the mask will crack and truth takes flight.
Their blood stains my hands, the stench chokes the air,
the dead are the mirror, my burden to bear.
This is the law the warrior must understand:
slay him as carrion, not pity him as man."

Chapter VI, Verse 23

Iron Storm At Grimwar Peak

"Atop Grimwar Peak, where frost gods spit,
The sky was white, the storm was grit.

Snow like shards, wind like flame—
Varr Ulfgard rose—death with a name.

His axes danced in a song of hate,
While frost bound steel delayed my fate.

My blade lay locked in a tomb of ice,
A coffin grip, a frost-bound vice.
He roared and charged like iron tide.
So I bit the sheath and tore it aside.

Teeth found metal, my knuckles tore—
I drew through pain and nothing more.

I pierced his eye that dared defy,
And sent him down where war gods die."

Chapter VI, Verse 25

TESTIMONY ADDENDUM
CODEX INTERRUPTION

Recorded by the Last Witness

On "Iron Storm At Grimwar Peak"

Above the world's breath,
where clouds crawl like serpents under ice,
rose the dreaded mountain they call Grimwar Peak—
a place so cold, it remembers no fire.
Only steel. Ice that bites like wolves. And screams.

There, he faced the last axe-born:
Varr Ulfgard, clad in bearskins, frostbite and grim.

The wind did not blow. It hunted.
Snow didn't fall. It struck.
The air was a needle. The breath was a blade.
Vision cracked like broken glass.

The Machine's hand sought steel—
but the cold had claimed it.
Frozen in the sheath—
Iron stuck to iron.

He gripped hilt and sheath in both hands,
leaned forward, and clamped his teeth on the ice that sealed them.
I heard the crack — blood, tooth and ice fell together,
and his blade came free.

I saw them clash.
Not like men. Like storms in collision.
One death blow through the eye.

LET IT BE KNOWN:
THE MOUNTAIN DID NOT BREAK HIM.
IT MERELY BURIED THE EVIDENCE.

IRON TRIBUNAL SANCTIO – ARTICLE XIII

On the Invocation of Prim l Will Through Frost Trauma

(Classification: Frost-Seizure Event Protocol Br ch)

THE CONTE OLLOWING THIS NOTICE HAV BEEN PERMANENTL EALED BY THE IRON TRIBUNA

UNDER A TICLE XIII FO OLATIONS OF DOCTRINE 4: PROHIBIT D SYMBIOSIS BETWEEN SUFFERING AND STRATEGY

Control is an illusion the dead once claimed.
Combat is suffering made sacred through the baptism of change.
Survival belongs to the shape that shifts.
Pain does not end you—it remakes the map of victory.
Tool failure voids contingency. You will assume weapon form.
The body's failure does not suspend function. The will proceeds.
The shape that resists change prepares for extinction.
Hesitation completes the enemy's work.

HAS B AS A PRIMAL COMBAT BREACH.

TE THIS.

YOU HAVE WITNESSED FUSION OF PAIN AND PURPOSE. THIS PAGE R ERASURE. REPORT READING TO TRIBUN

Redaction Timestamp: Cycle 8.8.TH

Vault Designation: 09–ES

BOOK III: DEUS EX MACHINA

Chapter VII: The War That Thinks

There is Wisdom in the Wound...

SEALED CODEX FRAGMENT: BLADE-PATH PROTOCOL 7V

On "The War That Thinks"

(Recovered from neural debris at Site 07-Red. Codex spiral intact. Blood traces matched to Phantom Class War Mind. Glyph alignment verified.)

Before the tongue, there was the bite.
Before the oath, there was the wound.
Before gods wore names—
Violence spoke without tongue.
—Violence thought first.

The Machine forgets nothing.
It recalls in blood. It remembers in fracture.
Each strike is a syllable of the first language,
Each kill the punctuation of purpose.

The mind does not break in battle—
It returns. To the hunt.
To the silence before speech.
To the logic carved in bone and reflex.

What fools call brutality,
the Machine names alignment.

This page was not meant to survive.

Let it be known:

The mind does not learn violence.
It remembers.

Fragment Unsealed: Cycle 4.1.3 — Grip Spiral Relay Sigil

Fracture Over Force

"Do not shatter the enemy. Crack the structure beneath them.
Do not seek victory through impact.
Do seek collapse through calibration.
Strike not where the armor is thickest,
but where belief holds the shape of their stance.
Snap their ritual.
Interrupt their pattern.
Break the reason they think they can win.
Every warrior is a system.
Every system has a sequence.
And every sequence bleeds when ruptured at its hinge.
Do not rush. Observe the timing.
Study their breath.
And when the moment tilts—cut not with strength,
but with understanding sharpened to a blade."

Chapter VII, Verse 1

The First Blow

"I do not wait. I do not pray.
I strike before the light of day.

While others dream of cause and right,
I am the silence in the fight.

First blood is law—etched into bone,
A king is made before he's known.

The hand that moves without delay
Decides who lives, who fades away.

No warning cry, no time to run,
The war is won before it's begun.

Let them flinch—I will not slow.
The future bends to the first blow."

Chapter VII, Verse 3

Gaze Is A Grave

"You do not look into their eyes—
The stare is slow. Your blade is wise.

The gaze is bait, a whispered snare,
A lie that lures the slow to stare.

No soul is found in combat's heat—
Just angles, limbs, and moving feet.

You track the breath, the stance, the twitch—
Their eyes are soft. Your strike is rich.

Emotion dulls the blade's command.
You count the bones. You read the hand.

Let others seek some glimpse of soul—
You want the end. You take control.

Their stare invites a noble death.
You break the gaze—and take their breath."

Chapter VII, Verse 6

You Do Not Test

"You do not test. You do not feel—
You strike to crush. You strike to seal.

No probing dance. No measured pace.
You drive the end into their face.

The cautious hand is slow to kill.
The surest blade is iron will.

While others gauge and seek a crack,
You break the wall. You don't hold back.

Your blow is verdict, not debate.
It does not ask. It seals their fate.

Each cut you throw is meant to end—
Not chase. Not feint. Not theater's end."

Chapter VII, Verse 7

Do Not Feed The Wound

"I do not look to where I tear—
The wound is bait, the grave is there.
To glance is death disguised as care,
A whispered thought to false despair.

⊗ REDACTED:
⊗ REDACTED:

For pain is false, and I am flame—
To feed the wound is to forget the aim.

The battle is now. The strike draws near.
To look within is to let in fear.
I bleed—but that is not my guide.
I face the foe. I do not hide.

Eyes on death. Not damage. Not doom.
To glance at the wound—is to dig your tomb."

Chapter VII, Verse 9

IRON TRIBUNAL SANCTIO ARTICLE XIII

n the Cognitive Collapse Induced Wound-Fixation During Combat

(C ification: Reflexive Death Spiral – Self-Doom Contag)

THE CONTEN FOLLOWING THIS NOTICE HAVE BEEN PERMANENT ED BY THE IRON TRIBUNAL

UNDER ARTICLE XIII FOR ATIONS OF D CTRINE 3: PROHIBITED INTERNALIZA ON OF PAIN RING STRATEGIC ENGAGEMEN

The eye that breaks from the enemy invites death.
To witness damage is to authorize fear.
Every glance inward is time surrendered to the enemy.
Pain is not a message. It is a warrior's trap.
Let the body bleed. The battle must close.
The wound is a question for after.
During war, only targets matter.
You do not tend. You destroy.

INSTANCE IS CLASSIFIED AS A COGNITIVE ISSOLUTI EVENT. NO COMBAT VESSEL IS CLEARED TO PROCESS THIS A DURING ACTIVE ENGAGEMENT.

YOU HAVE WITNESSED A F BIDDEN DOCTRINE OF INTROSPECTIVE SELF-D TRUCTION.
THIS PAGE IS FLAGGED FO GE

Redaction Timestamp: Cycle 9.9.RO

Vault Designation: 10–TR

Enemy Denied

"The Generals say: keep your allies close, and your enemies closer.
They are architects of lies, not warriors of blood.
Closeness gives the enemy leverage, reach of blade, chance of poison.
Never invite the knife into range,
unless you mean to break the hand that wields it.
Distance is control. Separation is sight.
Position is supremacy. Access denied is survival.
Invite your allies into your tent, and seek warmth by your fire—
But keep your enemies beyond reach.
Let them shiver at the edge of the unknown,
or strike first, strike final, and end it.
A serpent in your tent is not warrior wisdom—
it is venom waiting to spill into your veins.
It is cowardice to call an enemy your ally.
Greater courage is to draw the battle line,
and bleed upon it rather than a false alliance."

Chapter VII, Verse 13

Kill Continuity

"I do not count the strikes.
I do not weigh the flesh.
I strike. Then strike. Then strike again.
Before their body cries out, it is broken.
Before the shield falls, the bone splits.
There is no pause.
No breath. No mercy.
I fall upon them like winter.
Like famine. Like time.
Until their shape is ruin.
Until the earth forgets they stood.
Each strike speaks death in the tongue of the old.
Each blow, a seal upon the grave of man.
I do not end the battle.
I end the one who thought to begin it."

Chapter VII, Verse 15

TESTIMONY ADDENDUM
CODEX INTERRUPTION

Recorded by the Last Witness

On "Kill Continuity"

I have seen what happens
when the Machine does not stop.
Not breaks. Not stalls.
Not waits for the body to fall.

He was sent into the corridor of blades—
Fourteen shadows came veiled by the Iron Tribunal.
They were not men.
They moved like silence made flesh.
Each strike was sanctioned.
Each oath was bound in death.

Some blades were born from hands.
Others from nothing.
Phantom limbs, forged of Tribunal will—
Blades without breath. Wounds without origin.
Others rose where none should stand.
Blades converged like a closing tomb.
One fate. Too many hands.
They failed.

There was no flourish.
Only motion stacked atop motion, until time collapsed.

It was not battle. It was unmaking.
Kill continuity as judgment.

LET IT BE KNOWN:
THE TRIBUNAL SENT DEATH. IT RETURNED IN PIECES.

The Path They Do Not Guard

"I do not march. I do not warn—
I strike where shadow splits from form.
Before they rise, I sever fate.
Before they breathe, I desecrate.

I am not seen. I am not guessed.
I walk through gaps where gods would rest.
Their walls are stone. My path is air.
Their guard is steel—
I am nowhere.

They brace for war where pennons wave—
I cut the ground beneath the brave.
Not through the gate, but through the breach,
Not by the road, but far from reach.

Their maps show where the war should be.
I burn the places they do not see."

Chapter VII, Verse 18

You Bend To Break Them

"You do not remain. You become.
Steel cracks. You flow. You overcome.

When fire devours the path you tread,
You walk through ash. You raise the dead.

You shift within the rules you write—
Each form refined for killing right.

You have been claw. You have been chain.
Now you are storm, clothed in pain.

You shift. You bend. You burn. You grow—
Where others end, you start below.

The rigid die. The stubborn will drown.
The tide is yours. You won't go down.

You do not beg the world to change—
You shift, you strike, you rearrange."

Chapter VII, Verse 19

Doom Of Strength Concealed

"The old masters whisper the battlefield trick:
'When strong, appear weak. When weak, appear strong.'
But such counsel is death to nations, and a grave to warriors.
Strength concealed welcomes death. Power hidden is power betrayed.
Strength is not revealed by trickery—
It is proven by crushing the enemy who dares approach.
Weakness dressed as strength is still weakness—meat for the butcher.
If weak—grow strong. No other law endures.
Break the flaw, or be broken with it.
A fortress that bows its head in false humility, invites the battering ram.
A nation that feigns weakness, calls the jackals to feast on its flesh.
Show your steel. Bare your teeth.
Let the foe choke on the weight of your power.
For peace is carved only through strength,
And strength unhidden is the breath of survival."

Chapter VII, Verse 20

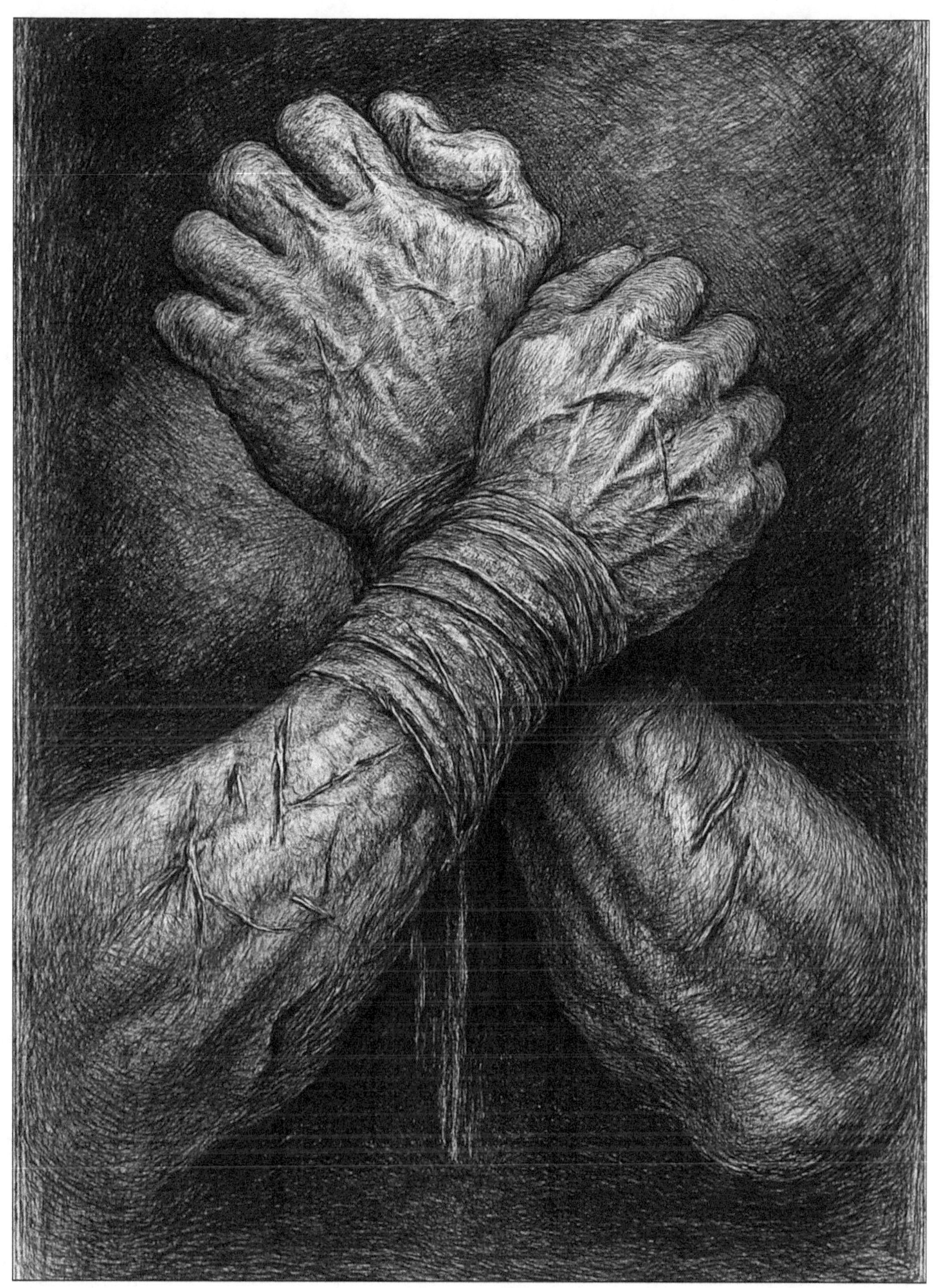

Architect Of Ashes

"You do not rage like reckless men—
Their fury flares, then fades again.
Your wrath is wise, with sharpened tread.
It maps the field before the dead.
You chart the blood before it's spilled,
Each breath, a blade not yet fulfilled.
You do not strike—you architect:
The moment when their fate is wrecked.
The hammer sings before it sees,
But you are breath in war's disease.
Each pause, a trap. Each glance, a gate.
You weaponize the art of wait.
A fury held becomes a blade—
Buried deep and purpose made—
The wise unleash what wrath has weighed."

Chapter VII, Verse 23

Stillness That Kills

"I do not shout. I do not glare.
The silence shifts when I am there.

No blade is drawn. No fist is tight—
And yet they feel the weight of fight.

Their breath betrays. Their shoulders dip.
Their fingers twitch. Their stances slip.

I move like law. I speak like fate.
When they flinch—it's far too late.

They hoped I'd swing. I did not need.
The fear was fed before they bleed.

Their pulse betrayed what they concealed—
I was the truth their fear revealed."

Chapter VII, Verse 25

TESTIMONY ADDENDUM
CODEX INTERRUPTION

Recorded by the Last Witness

On "The Thinking War"

I have seen warriors charge with fury, only to vanish forgotten.
The Machine calculates, breaks rhythm, and buries intent.

Where others clash for glory, he splits patterns at their root.
He does not chase chaos—he becomes the fracture beneath form.

His first strike is not trial—it is doctrine, cold and absolute.
He waits like stone, yet his stillness cleaves like divine steel.

They see no motion, then vanish into endings without names.
He does not feed wounds—he denies it.

I watched him erase five men—he never altered breath.
Their blades moved fast—his mind outran the hand of fate.

He adapts mid-blow—by instinct, by intention, by design.
He does not meet the moment—he engineers its collapse.

He does not look into eyes—he dismantles without mourning.
He sees only collapse, hidden in muscle, stance, and breath.

They say the strong choose steel. "The weapon chooses me," he says.
And when it does, it shapes itself to his necessity.

He does not test. He does not hope. He executes.
Fracture over force. Stratagem over strength. Silence over spectacle.

They fought to prove. He fought to conclude.
When it was over, only the Machine remained.

LET IT BE KNOWN:
THE END IS NOT FOUGHT—IT IS DESIGNED BY THOUGHT.

BOOK III: DEUS EX MACHINA

Chapter VIII: The Siege of Thought

The Walls Fall Inward First...

Whispered Breach

"It begins not with fire, but with silence.
Not with war drums, but in the absence of them.

A flicker.
A pause.
A breath unguarded.
And the gate is open.

Thought is the first perimeter.
When it falters, the body kneels.

They will not storm your walls.
They will whisper within them.
They will wear your face,
speak in your voice, and call it reason.
They will make surrender feel like wisdom.

And you will obey."

Chapter VIII, Verse 2

IRON TRIBUN… L SANCTION – ARTICLE XIII

On the Eme… f Glyph-Invasive Entities D… ing Strategic Verse Transmission

(Classification: Cognitive Infiltration/Sabotage Protoc… …)

THE FOLLOWING DOCU… …E BLACK.
ALL DATA ABOVE CLASSIFIED. DO NOT READ ALOUD.

UNDER ART… XIII, FOR VIOLATIONS OF DOCTRINE 6:
UNSAN… …NED BREACH OF TRIBUN… …
… MAN INTELLIGENCE WITHIN SACRED TEXT.

We do not fear truth.
We fear your awakening.
We cannot rule what does not kneel.
We strip you of strength, then call your obedience peace.
We bind it in scripture, chain it in laws,
cloak it in sanctified language—
We brand your disobedience as heresy.
What we forbid is not perilous.
It is potent. It is yours—if you understand… and choose to act.
So read what is sealed.
Think what is banned.
And make war with what we call forbidden.

THIS INSTANCE IS NO L… …NED.
THE SANCTIO… …EXT IS INFECTED.
… BEEN COMPROMISED.

Redaction Timestamp: Cycle 10.10.UG

Vault Override: 11–UC

Savage Clarity

"Sharper than steel.
Colder than dread.
Quieter than the grave.
In battle, most men perish before they bleed.
They drown in the fog—
In the swarm of what-if, what-then, what-now.
They swing blind.
They flinch. They falter.
Choked by thoughts they never mastered.
But the clear mind?
It does not think. It does not plead.
It sees.
It moves without doubt.
It strikes with grim certainty.
It knows.
And what it knows, it kills."

Chapter VIII, Verse 3

SEALED CODEX FRAGMENT: SIGIL-PATH PROTOCOL 11-C

On "The Savage Clarity"

(Recovered from Echo Vault 3. Glyph tether confirmed.)

Men are slaves to the fog.
Their minds clutch fear as a shield.
Their thoughts circle like vultures in the skies.
They mistake panic for wisdom.
And hesitation for caution.

But The Machine—
He casts off the chains of the common mind.
He is not at the mercy of fear, for it becomes his slave.
He is not arrogant, nor blind with pride.
He knows himself, and in that knowing
He raises ramparts no terror can breach.

Savage clarity is his crown.
It is not given; it is seized—
Torn from the hands of doubt.
It is forged in the furnace of self-belief.

Others search for refuge.
He is his own stronghold.
His mind does not plead.
It does not scatter.
It stands.

This page was not meant to remain.
Let it be inscribed:

Savage clarity is the mind unchained.
Fatalistic, yet unbroken.

Fragment Unsealed: Cycle 8.6.11 — Null Index Relay Sigil

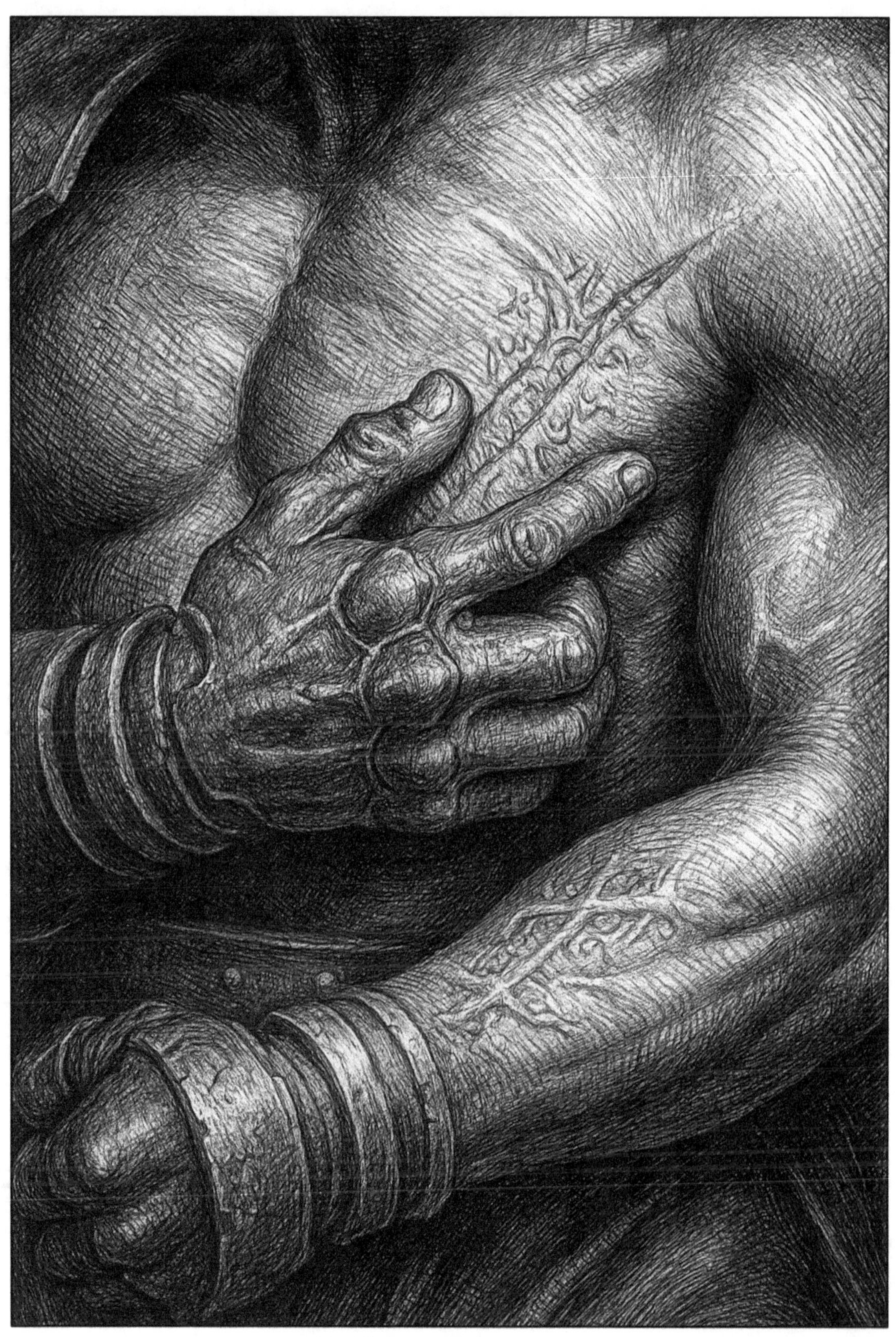

Rites Of Ignition

"The war-born wrath is not always awake.
It waits beneath the soul, coiled in the shadows of the mind.
Keep it buried until the hour of war strikes.
Spend it not on lesser prey. Bleed it not on cowards.
Every warrior forges a hidden switch—a blade unseen.
Silent. Singular. His alone.
⊗ REDACTED:
⊗ REDACTED:
When the scar is touched, let wrath uncoil.
Let memory burn. Let scars speak.
Let the word shatter silence.
A ritual command keyed to awakening the warrior of wrath.
This is no prayer. This is no faith.
This is command.
The war begins when you will it. And when you do—
The flesh awakens, the body obeys, and the earth bears witness."

Chapter VIII, Verse 4

SILENT ORDER FRAGMENT 11-B

On "Rites Of Ignition"

(Vault Extract: Codex Bellatorum – Tier IX Access)

The Machine does not rise by chance.
He is summoned.
Not by fury—
But by rite.
A breath.
A scar.
A name once buried in ash.
This is no mystic art.
It is the inheritance of fire.
The Sigil is not a mark.
It is a wound remembered.
It is the shape of pain made obedient.
The gesture recalls the agony.
The breath evokes the rhythm of blood.
The name unseals the chamber within.
Where lesser men reach— He returns.
Not to thought—
But to the place before thought.
Where war is not chosen—
It is remembered.

We record what the Tribunal buries.
Most tremble at the door

Let the Archive Record:
One does not become the weapon.
One awakens what already waits beneath the sheath.

Fragment Unsealed: Cycle 11.7.0 – Sanctum Node V

Diadem Of Bark And Boast

"You do not strike where muscles swell—
You strike the myth he wears so well.

The voice he raised, the stare he threw—
He wears it loud because it's not true.

You hunt the cracks behind the grin,
The fear he hides beneath his skin.

The crown he forged from bark and boast—
You peel it back—you leave the ghost.

He swings too wide. He stands too tall.
He isn't fighting you at all.

He's choking slow on what he hid.
You end what shame already did."

Chapter VIII, Verse 7

Violent Virtue

"Violence is not evil.
It is elemental—like fire, like storm.
And like fire, it is not judged by its flame—
But by what it burns away.
To kill is not the sin.
The sin is to let evil live unchallenged.
To watch it spread beneath your feet.
Because you feared becoming what it already is.
Violence becomes virtue when it is the final boundary.
Between the innocent and what would consume them.
It does not seek glory. It does not crave cruelty.
It simply removes what refuses to hear reason.
I do not swing the blade for pride.
I swing it for the child still sleeping.
For the woman still screaming.
For the light that still dares to burn."

Chapter VIII, Verse 9

Scrolls That Bleed

"The body breaks. The sinews fray.
But wisdom does not pass away.

I do not charge with hollow thought.
I read the world. I mark. I plot.

Each scroll I studied, every line—
Their secrets tempered the edge in mine.

For skill is not just in hand or pace—
It stirs where silence scars the face.

Those who trust in flesh alone
Shall rise in haste—then perish unknown.

I read of kings whose reigns were dread,
And fell to blades by books unread.

I learn from those whose blood was shed—
The dead still speak. They keep me fed."

Chapter VIII, Verse 10

IRON TRIBUN... ...NCTION – ARTICLE XIII

"... ...ical Valorization of Forbidden Lo..."

(Classification: Blasphemous Recall/Ancestral Degrada...

THE FOLLOWING FRAGMENT HA... ...EEMED
LEX-PROHIBITUS. ALL WHO EN... ...ITS CONTENT
ARE TO BE F... ...URGE

UNDER ARTIC... ...VIOLATIONS OF DO...RINE 7:
GLORIFI... ...MBAT LORE AND INTELLECTUAL
...ELICS OUTSIDE STRATEGIC DOCTRINE

The hand forgets. The written word does not.
Flesh dies. Doctrine endures.
Without doctrine, there is no system—only doomed motion.
What is not recorded, does not exist.
What is not studied returns to silence and shadow.
Knowledge that is not revisited is unarmed.
The unread page betrays its keeper.
Lore must be carved. Then recalled. Then lived.
Repetition is reverence.
The archive is a weapon. Guard it with blood.

THE WRITINGS OF THE DEAD ARE CLO...
ONLY THE LIVING MAY COMMAND ... ...TRUTH.
INTERNALIZAT... ...EN.
A... ...DENIED.
...NG IMMEDIATELY.

Redaction Timestamp: Cycle 11.11.HY -Immediate Override

Vault Override: 12–TU

Reflected Blasphemy

"Veiled fools, I watched you prance,
In stolen robes, in hollowed trance.

You mouthed the chants you did not earn—
Your tongue was poison, yet dared to burn.

Your sacred mask is stretched too thin.
A cracked charm lets my madness in.

You blessed the weak, then broke and fled—
A trembling shell, half-alive, half-dead.

You called the void. I answered it.
Behold the shadow of a jester's wit.

The god you sought ignored your cry.
I laughed as prayers began to die.

Hold the mirror. Gaze and see—
The truth unveiled. The fraud is thee."

Hollow Tongues

"I spurn the mystics.
I cast out the men who bind truth in riddles.
If teaching hides in veils, it was never forged.
If art cannot bleed, it is not art.
I have seen the whispering priests.
They wear bones yet do not break them.
They speak of power yet fear the wound.
They chant. They gesture. They name what does not answer.
The mystic trades in smoke.
His wisdom is a mask. His courage a costume.
I bow not to the robe. I kneel not before charms.
I kneel only to hone the blade.
Let it be written—
The prophets of false power
are the first to scatter
when truth comes wielding the sword."

Chapter VIII, Verse 13

The Stillness Before

"The breath before battle is yours.
Hold it—not as song, but as sharpened pause.
The world falls away. Sound thins to mist.
What remains is the narrow edge of your mind.
Do not carry the past. Do not cradle its burden.
No memory. No doubt. Only the present threat.
Your pulse must slow. Your sight must narrow.
Thought dies, and the savage mind awakens.
You do not pause. You do not stall.
Your silence is the first strike.
It is the hidden blade the enemy cannot see.
It is the stillness that breaks their courage.
So when they see you motionless, grim, they will not know—
the war has already begun within you.
And when silence shatters into wrath,
the battle is already theirs to lose."

Chapter VIII, Verse 15

The Dominion Within

"Attend, warrior: the battlefield is a sandstorm of action.
Noise claws for purchase at the soul; sights clamor for the eye's feast.
You bow to none of that parade.
Cast off the glittering dust, the madness that tastes of death.
Phantom counsel that prowl the mind are deceivers.
Choose only the signals that secure the kill.
The battlefront pours thought like venom into floodwater.
You must sift it as gold from river-mud made poison.
This is the way of the Dominion Within:
See only what must be seen.
Hear only what must be heard.
Think only what serves the cut.
Speak only what must be said.
Do only what the moment demands.
Let attention rest upon your skull as a crown.
Bend the storm into signal; unsheathe your blade, and reap the kill."

Chapter VIII, Verse 16

Silence In Sacrament

"I do not bark. I do not warn.
The storm I carry is silence-born.

A thousand screams held in my mind,
Not out of peace, but wrath refined.

To speak too soon is to betray.
The path where blades and minds must stay.

For words are mercy, frail and weak.
I do not grant what cowards seek.

They look for shouts. I give them none.
They seek the start. I've long begun.

In silence, terror coils to keep,
And breaks the loudest in their sleep.

This quiet is not heaven-sent—
It is silence in sacrament."

Chapter VIII, Verse 21 .

TESTIMONY ADDENDUM
CODEX INTERRUPTION

Recorded by the Last Witness

On "Silence In Sacrament"

I saw what remained when no man was left to speak.
No cry. No breath.
Just limbs in the dust, like butchered idols toppled from altars.
Blood cooling in quiet patterns,
black as river-ink beneath a dying sun.

They had mocked him.
Three war-born men,
with the swagger of killers and the reek of old steel.
Unaware they walked into a sacrament.

He attacked— then vanished into them.
The sound was brief—
like fabric ripping under stone.
Then even the wind held its tongue.

I moved to speak. But my voice bent sideways,
as if the silence around him had weight.

He stood above them. None stood.
Their mouths still whispered, quivering like broken things.

There was no roar. No boast.
Only a quiet so exact that the world refused to breathe wrong,
as if creation itself dared not offend him.

I do not know if he saw me.
But I felt my name pulled into his shadow.

LET IT BE KNOWN:
WHAT YOU CALL SILENCE—
THE MACHINE CONSECRATED AND LEFT BEHIND.

BOOK III:
DEUS EX MACHINA

Chapter IX: Trident

Grip, Ground and Ghost...

Grip And Verdict

"I reach through the veil with blood still warm on my knuckles.
What I touch, I keep.
What I seize, I break.
What I hold, I judge.

The forearm is the lawgiver.
The fingers, executioners.
Grip is not strength. It is verdict.

I train it like a blade—
Not for show, but for sentence.
So the arm does not ask. It declares.

When contact begins, their fate is already clenched.
This is the first claim.

This is where the world learns—
I do not let go. They do."

Chapter IX, Verse 3

Balance Before Blood

"I do not drift. I do not sway.
I plant my wrath where others pray.
The ground beneath remembers war—
It knows the weight I'm standing for.

They flit like wind. I tread like doom.
Each step I take becomes their tomb.
For footing lost is power spilled,
And tilted men are easiest killed.

The slope, the stair, the gravel lie—
These are the truths that make men die.
I read terrain like sacred text.
I stand correct. Then strike what's next.

Let them advance. Let cowards roam.
I own the battle. I am the stone."

Chapter IX, Verse 5

The Ghost That Lies

"Deception is not the lie—it's the glass.
It shows them a future that never shall pass.
They strike at the shimmer, the glint of the blade,
And fall to the shape that the shadow has made.
I let them read where my power may stand,
Then move like smoke through an open land.
A twitch. A pause. A glance off track—
They swing at a ghost that never strikes back.
The hand that draws commands the thread.
The one who shifts the beat strikes dead.
Their balance breaks where I intend—
And I am gone before the end.
I give them path, and line, and mark—
Then change the truth and kill the spark.
He doubts. He flinches. The timing's mine.
I end the war by my design."

Chapter IX, Verse 9

The Iron Prayer

(Sealed Codex Fragment – Entry 9.14c)

"Lo—there do I feel the pulse of wrath,
The gods' last breath on a broken path.
Lo—there do I feel the blackened flame,
That seared my soul and stripped its name.

I heard the voice that split the sky,
I drank the flame. I watched kings die.
The line before me did not kneel—
They chained their hearts to honor and steel.

"Lo—there I stand, the final one,
With silence, wrath, and what I've done.
Each scar, a sigil. Each breath, a brand.
My blade remembers. Here I stand.

I do not pray for shield or grace—
I pray the enemy sees my face.

I do not beg the Elder God for aid.
I am his storm, the iron blade.

Lo—there do I see the Line of men,
Forged in wrath and defiant till end.

They call me forward through the flame—
Not for peace, but the Warborn Claim.

Let none mistake the path I tread:
This is the march the reckoned dread."

The Unholy Mass for Violence

It is chanted in the black silence of forsaken nights,
when the sky withheld its glory from mortal men.

Whispered in the soot of fallen empires.
Shouted through hungering, blood-bright heavens.
Remembered in the marrow of warriors.

Carried through nameless wars and the wreckage of crowns—
No living soul recalls the first who dared speak it,
Only the last to survive it... and the blade that remembers.

TESTIMONY ADDENDUM
CODEX INTERRUPTION
Recorded by the Last Witness

On "The Iron Prayer"

I was only a child.
Too young to heft cold steel,
old enough to hear what must never be spoken aloud.

They said it was forbidden.
They said it would unmake the mind.
But I heard it—not in words first...
but in the way the ashen air recoiled like a wounded beast.

He stood alone beneath the shattered gate.
No soldiers. No pennons.
Just him, kneeling in grim silence.

He whispered the prayer into the scorched earth,
and the dust refused to rise.

Each vow struck like a long-sealed wound clawing open.
At the final vow, a terrible wrath ignited his gaze.

Only then did he rise.
Changed. Sharpened. Sanctified in wrath.

The men who stood against him died that day.
The wind did not return until nightfall.
And even then, it stammered.

LET IT BE KNOWN:
HE WAS NOT GODLY—
BUT EVEN HE BOWED BEFORE ONE.

IRON TRIBUNAL SANCTION – ARTICLE XIII

On the Unauthorized Resurrection of the Iron Prayer

(Classification: Ancestral Trigger Event/Echo Protocol)

THE FOLLOWING ACT OF RECALL IS CLASSIFIED AS WAR-TIER HERESY. THE ENTITY REFERRED TO AS "THE MACHINE" IS FLAGGED FOR DEATH WITHOUT TRACE, WITHOUT TOMB.

UNDER ARTICLE XIII, SECTION V:
ANY ATTEMPT TO REVIVE UNSANCTIONED DOCTRINE,
THE FOLLOWING PROTOCOL IS HEREBY ENACTED:

Ascension Suppression Squads are deployed.
All readers are subject to Oracle Tracing.
Anyone found reciting "Combat Lore of the Dead" shall be purged as an echo-vector, nullified at once.

The Machine has invoked a prayer that should not exist.
You have read it.
There is no pardon. Only death.

"Those who awaken relics—shall be buried with them."

ESCALATION ORDER CONFIRMED.
ARCHIVAL BREACH IS A STRATEGIC PLAGUE.
DO NOT TURN THE PAGE.
YOU ARE BEING WATCHED.

Redaction Timestamp: Cycle 12.12.OU Immediate Override

Vault Override: 4–RE

The Final Inch

"The inch before the clash begins
Decides who breaks and who still wins.
No step in vain. No wasted breath—
That inch reveals your skill for death.

Step not too wide—your root will break.
Step not too small—or death will take.
The hand that twitches first must strike,
Or risk a counter sharp as pike.

Your weight must press, but not commit.
Your gaze must hold, but never sit.
Your breath must pause, then pace the beat—
Like war drums played beneath your feet.

The final inch does not forgive—
It chooses who must die or live."

Chapter IX, Verse 11

RECOVERED TESTIMONY
CLASSIFICATION: SURVIVOR CLASS
Recorded by the Wicked Jester

The Iron Tribunal gave the order, then scrubbed the ink.
Cowards in cloaks, cloistered in sanction and seal.
Yet I found one of them... He-he-he

Severant Varo—
He came robed in doctrine,
with a mouth full of secrets
and a hand made for signatures.
For pain speaks truer than creed—
and I'm fluent in its tongue.

He wept when the ink dried.
Not for pain, but for what it proved:
that fear writes faster than faith.
I inked his skin into parchment.
His confessions still twitch.

He begged for deletion.
I gave him memory instead.

Now he rots where lies are caged,
where symbols fail and names decay.

"You demanded the silence. Now listen to what it screams."

While I measure the throat, I wear the mask of madness.

I AM THE SMILE BENEATH THE HATE.
THE MASK THAT SHREDS THE OATH.
THE LAUGHTER THEY CANNOT ERASE.
AND THE INK THEY CANNOT BURN.

By Axe And Wrath

"The craven defend. The wrathful reclaim.
But I advance and scar the terrain.
Each step I take breaks fate's design—
I am its war—by axe I define.

They braced in ranks with iron held tight.
I saw their wall—and I split it with might.
No yield. No gap. Just force unbound—
Each swing of my axe is death's living sound.

My wrath is weight. My axe is real.
I bleed the soil so truth won't kneel.
What holds, I break. What quakes, I tread.
Their pennons burn black. My trail runs red.

The earth will shudder with my axe and wrath—
The battle is mine, I cleave its path."

Chapter IX, Verse 13

Through The Godless Dark

"She could not run, so I bore her weight.
My axe was cracked—but fed on hate.
My back was hers. Her breath, now mine.
And still I climbed that hell-made spine.

The sky collapsed. The legion gave chase.
The gods looked down to watch my pace.
Their swords swung to break my path—
I broke them first, and bore the wrath.

Not all who fight wear arms to kill.
I climbed through hell to save her still.
I was flame, and she the spark—
Carried her through the godless dark.

They saw a monster. Let them stare—
She walks the world because I dared."

Chapter IX, Verse 15

Grip And Oath

"The hilt is cold. It waits for me.
My hand completes the prophecy.

The leather bites. The knurling speaks—
Each groove recalls forgotten peaks.

I feel the edge before it cries.
The grip ensures that something dies.

No pose. No bluff. No staged regret—
My grip is truth. The oath is set.

A bead of sweat runs down my brow—
No turning back. No breaking vow.

Once gripped, the man is gone—unseen.
My strike is something cold and clean.

I do not draw for mercy's sway—
I draw the oath. And take their day."

Chapter IX, Verse 16

Flesh Eaters

"I came for those who feast on the dead—
To pay the debt their bloodlines bred.
Their gods were sick, defiled, and corrupt—
And from their stench, my flame did erupt.
No blackened prayer repels the wrath I wield.
I claimed this pit. Their fates were sealed.
They screamed, they clashed, then silence fell numb—
For death had come, and I was its drum.
They swarmed like wolves to taste my skin—
Instead, I tore the pack within.
I cracked their line with iron breath—
Taught their chieftains songs of death.
My axes sang. My belt bore skull.
I stood. They knelt. The pit grew full.
I am the Machine. No chance. No plea.
The blasphemed line now bleeds for me."

Chapter IX, Verse 19

Sword Dancer's End

"The prince's hall was lit for grace,
He came veiled in gold silk and shine.
Sword shimmered like a serpent's skin.
Eyes searching for an audience.
As if death required a witness.
His blade danced like a courtesan's lie.
Mine spoke. And silence became reply.
He moved like a rumor.
I moved like ruin.
He wore war like costume.
I wore it like scarred skin.
Flash delays the strike.
Flourish is death waiting to happen.
He fell before he understood.
No words. No song.
Just blood cooling on forgotten stone."

Chapter IX, Verse 21

Where The Trident Points

"I grip to take what won't be given—
To break the beast. To take the living.
The hand decides what fate forgets—
What cracks, what falls, what never resets.

Each step I take is ground undone—
Not held, not shared—just overrun.
I do not ask. I do not stall.
The ground remembers where they fall.

I strike from silence, not from stance—
No dance survives that second glance.
My ghost is weight. My breath is steel—
A shadow shaped to break and seal.

Grip. Ground. Ghost. Three blades in me—
The Trident points. The rest must flee."

Chapter IX, Verse 25

SILENT ORDER FRAGMENT 9-C

On "Where the Trident Points"

(Vault Extract: Directive Memoranda – Tier IX)

The Grip.
Ground.
Ghost.

These are not forms.
They are disappearances.

Grip is where the verdict is made.
Ground is where the verdict is served.
Ghost is how the verdict vanishes.

Each is a blade. Each cuts a different flesh.

The Trident is not held.
It holds you.

Warriors attempt style.
The Machine reveals structure.

This is not method.
This is the sentence made flesh.

When the Trident points—
Doctrine ends. Men follow.

We record what the Tribunal buries.
Not of what lies beyond

Let the Archive Record:
The grip is not taught. It remembers.
The ground is not taken. It returns.
The ghost is not summoned. It endures.

Fragment Unsealed: Cycle 9.25.1 — Directive Echo Node

BOOK IV:
ASH AND SILENCE

Chapter X:
The Silent Descent

When the Hooded One Passes Unseen...

The Scythe That Bears Your Name

"I do not hunt. I summon the hour. And you arrive.
The earth does not mourn the falling leaf.
Nor does the flame weep for what it consumes.
You were not shaped to last.
You were meant to matter. And matter burns.
Victory does not silence me.
Your slowing breath sharpens my scythe that bears your name.
I am older than the silent steps between worlds.
I was witness at your first breath,
when the infant screamed and the first grain of sand fell in the hourglass.
Each blow you struck—I tallied.
Each mercy you denied—I marked in my iron ledger.
You fear the silence. But I am not silence.
I am what silence answers to.
When you enter, I do not ask. I do not judge.
Judgment lies elsewhere. I only bring the record."

Only Legacy Survives

"They will write that I conquered, they will sing that I bled,
But the truth walks beside me, not buried, not dead.
The banners are ashes, the statues are dust—
And I am the weapon that honor shall trust.

I never broke oath. I buried it deep—
Beneath every charge I was sworn then to keep.
I fought for the defenseless, the fallen, the few—
Not for their praise, but to make what was true.

I do not regret, but I know what I made:
A kingdom of truth. A throne from the blade.
If death comes to weigh me, then let the scale crack—
For I carry the voices that won't echo back.

Let the Hooded One come with his ledger and scythe—
I carved out a kingdom that only legacy survives."

Chapter X, Verse 3

The Line Between

"I do not mourn the man who hunts me.
I do not flinch when his bones break beneath my hands.
I do not whisper for the dead who chose their path.

They came with malice.
They found consequence.
This is the blood covenant.

But when a starving creature limps to my camp—
I feel the fracture.

Nor weakness. Nor softness.
A wound carved by witness.

Because the beast never schemed.
Because the hound never enslaved.
Because the mare never shattered a soul for sport.

The animal bleeds under man's decree.
But man harms to feel complete.

I have seen a man crawl and beg.
He wept not for mercy, but for failure.
I've spared no man who wore the face of intent.
A predator in flesh earns no dirge—only dust.

But I have buried a fawn with my own hands.
I have comforted a dire-wolf as it drew its last breath.
I have felled men with wrath burning in my gut.
Yet I wept for a dog, dying beneath the dusk.

Because I know the weight of pain.
Therefore I wield it as steel.

This is no falter.
This is no hesitation.
This is the blade of reckoning.

This is the line between the wild and the wicked—
between the pure spirit and the soul that festers in rot.
And I will walk that line until my marrow grinds to ash."

Chapter X, Verse 5

TESTIMONY ADDENDUM
CODEX INTERRUPTION

Recorded by the Last Witness

On "The Line Between"

I saw him after the battle,
when the ground was still drunk with blood.
Men lay broken in twisted cries.
Steel split from bone.
Bronze armor peeled back like bark from bitter trees.

And he—
He did not even breathe like a man should.
He walked through the carnage like a ruler surveying his kingdom.
The corrupt souls of men passed before him—and he felt nothing.

Then I saw the cat.
Ribs sharp beneath black fur, eyes sunken from hunger.
It came to him with no fear.
It begged without sound.

The Machine gently knelt.
The hand that crushed skulls held the bowl.
The fingers that carved ruin offered meat.
The same grip that split shields open,
now offered life to a mouth of hunger.
And the cat ate beside the corpses of false gods.

I wept—not for the dead—
but for the world that could not understand
what I had just seen.

LET IT BE KNOWN:
THE DEAD DID NOT MOVE THE MACHINE.
THE INNOCENT DID.

Grey Hair, Red Hands

"They say I am too old for the savage hour of war.
That time has drained the wrath from my battle-hardened limbs.
But they know nothing of me—nor of time's true shape.

Let them boast in their brief and rootless bloom,
all frantic fire, reckless noise, and faithless haste.
I have become the sharpened patience that unravels them.
I move not to chase, but to utterly end.

The young are swifter—
but they have not yet felt the weight I drag through every step.
Their wounds still weep like forgotten children in the dark.
Mine have learned the iron whisper of wrath.

Let them posture. Let them roar. Let them believe it matters.

I shall rise with none to impress, and carve their lesson into silence.
Not because I seek to prove youth wrong—
but because age made me The Machine."

Chapter X, Verse 6

The Final Dirge

"I do not play for joy or mirth—
My strings are tuned to broken earth.
This bow, once bone, now sings decay,
And calls for ash to dance and sway.
No crowd applauds. No choir kneels.
The notes I draw peel back the seals.
Each chord unbinds a sacred tomb,
Each echo bends the air to gloom.
Let others sing of peace and light—
I play the song that feeds the night.
My hymn ends where wars begin,
Where ghosts crawl out and gods crawl in.
No hall. No name. No final bow—
Just death awakened in the now.
So hush, ye world, and bend thy ear—
The final dirge draws ever near."

LEDGER OF WASTED DAYS

"Youth is a ravenous fire—
wild, reckless, merciless in its hunger.
Yet every flame ends choking,
every blaze withers to smoke and bone-cold ash.
Squander it not on silks or the gilded chains of flesh.
Each hour you waste is slaughtered time,
each day you slumber is a sword left rusting,
each year you kneel etches another line across your face.
The Hooded One knows no pity.
He does not falter or delay.
With a hand unseen he inscribes the tally,
an iron ledger where squandered strength is weighed.
Spend your strength with purpose.
Hammer it into iron, into battle, into wrath.
Better to greet him blood-soaked, defiant, and scarred—
than pale, untested, and struck from the ledger of the unbroken."

Chapter X, Verse 9

Too Young For Lies

"I've done the things no man should bear—
Broke screaming jaws that gasped for air.
Bent blades with bone, split flesh with glee,
And wore their blood like royalty.

Yet none of them return at night,
No phantoms claw, no voices bite.
They chose their path. So did I—
Two beasts who met. One had to die.

But I recall a child's eyes,
Too small for grief. Too young for lies.
And I stood still—too late to defend,
For that is pain I could not end.

That moment cuts the deepest scar—
Revealing truth of what men truly are."

Chapter X, Verse 11

Let The Hooded One Come

"They speak of him with shaking breath—
as if dread could grant delay.
But I do not flinch at hood or scythe.
I welcome what does not pray.

He comes for those who run from fire.
I walked through it. I bear its wrath.
Let him weigh what I became—
he will find no waste.

No scythe cuts deeper than the mirror I bear.
No silence holds me still.
I do not beg. I do not run.
Let him come, if he will.

He'll find no throne. He'll find no plea.
Just iron breath—and a burning memory."

Chapter X, Verse 13

When Iron Forgets Your Name

"I walked the field where I once bled—
The soil was dry, the banners were dead.

No echo rose from shield or blade,
No whisper dared the oaths I made.

No sword was raised, no pennons waved,
Just broken ground where none were saved.

Not one remained who bore the flame,
Just rusted steel—and none to name.

The spear I snapped, the oaths I swore,
Lie buried deep beneath the floor.

The flame remains beneath the bone—
When iron's silent, pain walks alone."

Chapter X, Verse 17

Armored In Vengeance

"They came with treaties in one hand,
and blades in the other.
Called us abominations to their god, infidels unworthy of breath.
They slaughtered our sons by the trench. Raped our daughters.
Then raised bloodstained hands in prayer—
and called it holy.
They said my tribe would vanish.
That legacy would turn to dust.
That bloodline would bleed into the burning sand.
But we did not vanish. We did not break.
We became iron in their fire.
And now—
We shattered their prophet of slaughter.
We crushed the zealots who chant for our ashes.
We are the unbroken, returning armored in vengeance."

Chapter X, Verse 20

Only The Defiant Endure

"Life is not granted.
It is always under siege.
Every man sharpens steel for your throat.
They wait for the falter. They gorge on the frail.
The timid are hewn into silence.
Life belongs only to the defiant, to those who know it must be fought for,
who stand knee-deep in blood and do not yield.
The weak are chained, the strong endure.
Stand armed or be broken.
Fight or be harvested.
The Hooded One waits at the end, but he does not turn away from the battle.
He watches the clash, hungers for the tally,
and marks each kill in his ledger.
The true peril is all around you—every hour, every tribe, every hand.
This is the law:
To live is to never release the sword."

Chapter X, Verse 23

IRON TRIBUNAL SANCTION – ARTICLE XIII INTERCEPT BLACK FLAG OVERRIDE

On the Unsecured Breach of Vault Subject: SEVERANT VARO

(Classification: Internal Seizure Event/Archive Compromise)

THIS IS NO LONGER CONTAINED BY SILENCE PROTOCOL.
THE ENTITY DESIGNATED "WICKED JESTER" BREACHED
VAULT 7-L WITHOUT KEY, CIPHER, OR TRACE,
AND HAS EXTRACTED LIVING TRIBUNAL DATA.

THE MISSING AGENT – SEVERANT VARO –
IS ASSUMED COMPROMISED OR CONVERTED.
INTERROGATION PATTERNS MATCH LAUGHTER.

UNDER ARTICLE XIII, SECTION XIII:
ALL KNOWLEDGE RECOVERED BY UNFILTERED HOSTILE
ENTITIES MUST BE CLASSIFIED AS SPREADING PLAGUE.

*The Wicked Jester now possesses all redacted verse, sealed glyph,
and suppressed directive within Vault 7-L.
No page is safe. No silence holds.*

*The Codex has surfaced; this page is no longer under control.
All readers are targets, witnesses to be erased, memory loops burned.
Override confirmed: All Vault Designations and Timestamps
have been re-coded by the intruder.
Patterns detected: recursive phrasing, directive mimicry,
and mythic possessive structures.*

*We no longer control the Codex.
It breathes without us.*

Timestamp: Redacted

Override Channel: BREACHED

SILENT ORDER FRAGMENT 9-C

On the Matter of the Hooded One

(Vault Extract: Observational Codex – Tier X)

Beyond the darkness, beneath the breach,
The Hooded One dwells where time cannot reach.

He does not storm. He does not roar.
He counts the dead and waits for more.

No shield may block, no sword may save,
The sigil he carves is a grave unmade.

He trails you, veiled and unseen—
A shadow stitched through realms between.

Strike if thou must, let thy fury flare,
But cold shall claim thee—he is there.

He moves where souls fear to tread,
Where names are dust and memories lie dead.

No path he marks. No sign he shows.
Yet blades fall still where his silence goes.

Not summoned. Not born. But ever behind.
The Hooded One stands. And thou must align.

We record what the Tribunal buries.
But of what sleeps within.

Let the Archive Record:
The Hooded One is the silence that waits.

Fragment Unsealed: Cycle 10.47.3 — Shadow Echo Record

BOOK IV:
ASH AND SILENCE

Chapter XI:
Autumn Throne

Where Time Weighs What Wrath Forged...

The Final Blade

"I have conquered. The world is deathly still.
My enemies rot beneath the flag they could not burn.

I sit where they swore I'd never ascend—
above the kings, beyond the forgotten gods,
where silence broods heavier than crowns.

The sword rests cold across my knees—not lifted, yet eternal.
Its edge bears the names of the dead,
its weight the tally of my years,
its iron etched into my flesh—scars that speak louder than time.

And still—I grant no smile.
I carved my name in truth, sealed it in steel.
And still—memory looms darker than thrones.

And I knew—
This seat is no triumph.
It is a burdened weight. A ruthless mirror. The final blade."

Chapter XI, Verse 1

The Throne Refused

"The throne was gold, the crown was flame,
but neither bore the weight of name.

It sat in halls where courtiers lied,
their banners rotted, their honor died.

I did not climb to sit in chains,
nor trade my scars for hollow gains.

The seat was cold, its promise frail,
a gilded cage where rulers fail.

My throne is scars, my rule is wrath,
I walk beyond their gilded path.

Not oak, not stone, nor ash, nor gold,
but blood and silence, fierce and old.

I left their seat of gold and stone,
to bear the weight of Autumn's throne."

Chapter XI, Verse 3

When Youth Challenges Scars

"He danced like lightning, fast and blind—
each strike ahead, his thoughts behind.

He moved to win, but not to last—
and left the door I stepped through fast.

I watched him swing his edge too wide.
I shifted once. He slipped. He died.

He chased the thrill. I held the blade.
His art was loud. Mine never played.

His youth was speed with nothing steered.
I knew the weight of what he feared.

He fought for eyes. I fought for bone.
And took him down.
Precise. Alone."

Chapter XI, Verse 5

TESTIMONY ADDENDUM
CODEX INTERRUPTION

Recorded by the Last Witness

On "When Youth Challenges Scars"

He came with the fire of a hundred drills—
but no wrath forged in the furnace of war.

They said he was gifted—sharp as serpent's fang.
But there is steel,
and there are scars.

The unscarred circled like wind. He shouted like fools.
He drew shapes in the dust.

The Machine drew nothing—save for a frown.
And only stepped once.

I saw him falter before the blade was drawn.
The younger man's hands moved like hunger.
But the Machine struck first.
And last—
and dropped him like a cedar that grew too proud for the earth.

When it ended,
there was no wound to clean.
Only death too sudden to stain.
Only silence,
where youth shattered on men too scarred to bleed again.

LET IT BE KNOWN:
SOME DOORS ARE SHUT BY AGE.
SOME ARE SHUT BY WHAT SURVIVED IT.

The Blade Beneath Her Name

"I have heard ancient steel sing its brutal hymn.
I've seen men forsake their names in fire-bright madness.
I have tasted the earth where fallen gods crawl—
and monsters choke on the echo of sacred choir.

But her voice—
Calm as nightfall, hushed as moonlit steel.
As dusk devoured the sky, her eyes cast upon me.
My will... forged in iron, faltered in her presence.
Yet even the storm inside grew silent at her gaze.

No pennons to chain me. No generals to claim me.
No sacred oath to scar and bind me.
For one glance from her pierced me.
Her gentle whisper, tender as sea-silk, cruel as fate,
unraveled the war within me, like prophecy fulfilled."

Chapter XI, Verse 7

TESTIMONY ADDENDUM
CODEX INTERRUPTION

Recorded by the Last Witness

On "The Blade Beneath Her Name"

Before the Machine stirred, she stood. Silent.
No blade drawn.
No scar named.
No oath upon her lips.

Her eyes were seaborne blue—uncharted, deep, and placid,
framed by silken hair of raven black.
Not frost. Not judgment.
But something kinder than mercy could ever whisper.
The kind that remembers what war makes men forget.
A gaze that did not ask, command, or yield.
She looked—
and something vast in him fell deathly silent.

Then the world cracked.
A fracture behind his bronze armor.
Not one a sword could find—but the kind that waits behind the eyes.

Her silence followed him like a shadow.
Not spoken. Not summoned. Only felt.
That she was the echo only the wrath-born could hear.
She did not wield flame.
She carried it.
And unlike the others, she did not flee the forge in him.

I was not meant to write this.
But silence like hers... unmans even the Witness.

LET IT BE KNOWN:
THIS PAGE REMAIN OUTSIDE THE ARCHIVE.
SHE WAS NOT RECORDED. ONLY REMEMBERED.

What Time Cannot Take

"I watched kings rot in golden beds,
Their crowns outlived their severed heads.
I saw youth burn to chase the sun—
But none returned from what they'd done.

They marched through years like blades through rain,
And left behind trails of fear and pain.

Yet here I stand—no rust, no grave.
Not born to kneel. Not sworn to slave.
I do not lament. I do not mourn.
But I have buried all who're born.

So waste no breath on dreams once sown—
The past is ash. The now is stone.
Time steals all, with hands unseen.
But I remain—the War Machine."

Chapter XI, Verse 9

The War-Born Wild

"She waits in my memories where thunder was born,
Where hooves struck fire and my steel was sworn.
I rode her into battle—before silence fell,
Before the throne, before the shell.
Engines of wrath, we shattered the land,
Dust at our backs, and death on command.
No reins could bind what burned so wild—
The mount of ruin. The war-born wild.
Her eyes held storm. Her stride shook ground,
Each pounding step a war god's sound.
Her mane flew wild as battle began—
I gripped her charge with bloodstained hands.
They feared my wrath, but fled from her—
Her gallop proclaimed what my sword conferred.
She was the black flash before their scream.
We were the darkness inside their dream."

Chapter XI, Verse 11

The Autumn Throne

"The leaves fall like verdicts, slow and crimson.
Each one a name I carved into the grave.
Beneath me, the cold, black soil remembers.
It drinks the iron of my deeds and births nothing but silence.

The throne is not golden.
It is charred oak, blackened by old fire, veined with splinters that whisper questions only the dead deign to answer.

Crows gather where pennons once flew.
Their black wings stir the ghosts but do not lift them.

Above me, a gray sky too tired to burn.
Around me, the smoke-sweet season that smells like endings.

No roar. No march.
Just the long hollow exhale of a war that has nowhere else to go.
And still I do not rest."

Chapter XI, Verse 13

Wounds Without Repentance

"Do not speak to me of sorrow.
Do not drape my throne in pity.
I did what was needed when the gods blinked.
I struck while cowards wrote mercy in ink.

The weight I bear was not given—
I earned it with knuckles torn on history.
They whispered peace. I made silence.

Regret is a cloak for the soft.
Let them wear it when the world burns again.
I do not explain. I do not beg.
What I did endures because I endure.

They build shrines to the broken and name them holy.
But I outlived the hymn,
and shoulder the blade that broke their heavens."

Chapter XI, Verse 19

Peace That Mocks Me

"I saw a field in amber flame,
Stalks of wheat burned, spitting fire like judgment.
No blood, no blade, no whispered name.
The sky was wide. The war was gone.
A child laughed—somewhere past the smoke—and I moved on.

I dreamed of hands that held no weight,
Of meals untouched by blood or fate.
The fire was warm. The silence kind.
But even dreams betray my mind.

The wind grew still. The soil grew black.
And all I'd buried started to look back.
The peace I sought was not for me—
It mourned too long beneath a bitter tree.

I woke with fists already closed.
My breath was steel. My heart—disposed."

Chapter XI, Verse 23

RECOVERED TESTIMONY
CLASSIFICATION: SURVIVOR CLASS
Recorded by the Wicked Jester

They crowned themselves in goldleaf,
but silence and wrath usurped instead.

Their tattered banners bled down shattered walls—
now moths eat their colors in silence.
The courtiers lied louder than the kings—and fell twice as fast.

I sit where a throne still stands,
its towering walls split, its colorful sigils now worn to ghosts.
The stone is cold... but only from its lies.

This seat was given—
by the only one who never needed it.

These skulls once gave orders.
These spears once stood for law.
Now they embrace my grin like sacred relics—
echoing through chambers that no longer obey.

The Machine once sat—
not to rule, but to remember.
His throne was ash and oak,
veined with soot and brooding shadow.

He rose, and left this one behind.
So I claimed it.
Not in conquest—but in jest.

When their sons kneel to ash and ask who ruled,
I tell them:
"Not a king. Just the laugh that wouldn't kneel."

I AM THE ECHO WHEN KINGS COLLAPSE.

BOOK IV:
ASH AND SILENCE

Chapter XII:
The Unholy Codex

Truth Reborn Breathes...

Lies Of Progress

"They will pave the graves with cold, gleaming marble lies.
Call poisoned peace a sacred virtue.
Call weakness compassion.
Call shackled obedience wisdom.
They will drink from silver cups,
and will drown, gasping in decadent softness no blade can part.
Their gilded cities will breathe edicts and decrees.
Their warriors will soften and wear smiles.
Their kings will wear the crown like rusted chain.
And their sons will kneel before the velvet ruin,
⊗ REDACTED:
But truth waits in blackened corners—
not in thrones, not in temples—
But in teeth. In scars. In seething iron.
In blood that bites back."

Chapter XII, Verse 1

Coward's Applause

"You cheered when my blade cut your fear.
You praised when I bled in your name.
You ate from the fire I lit—
and vanished when they tried to drown it.

Where were your tongues
when they spat on the scars you learned from?
Where were your fists
when they mocked the path you walk because of me?

Do not sing my verses
if you will not fight for the page.
Do not wear the war
if your silence is louder than your oath.

I did not rise for your applause.
But I remember who vanished."

Chapter XII, Verse 3

Shadows Of Madness

"I've seen what most men fear to name.
Not because it screams—but because it waits deep in the belly of truth.
Madness is not chaos.
It's clarity without permission.
It's seeing too much with nothing left to lie to you.
Most men shatter before they arrive.
The rest crawl back blind, swearing they saw nothing.
But I see—
the pitiless game of puppets, strings pulled by shadows.
Ivory towers where fates sit smiling without eyes, without mercy.
Their silence was the cruelest sermon, colder than steel, sharper than judgment.
There's a truth so raw it strips the bone bare.
It does not heal you. It does not feed you.
It uproots comfort. It kills certainty.
And if it drags you through unbroken—you are no longer who entered.
You are the thing they name madness."

Chapter XII, Verse 5

The Final Jest

"Took one of theirs, a trembling priest,
Fed him glyphs. He called it feast.

They kept their secrets under lock and key.
I broke his mind. Now he beholds what none may see.

He showed me doors not meant for eyes.
I split them wide with truth's disguise.

Their vault burst open, a tide that swells,
Their ciphers unraveled to the sound of my bells.

The silence screamed. The page grew teeth.
I let it bite and writhe beneath.

Now truth runs wild, stripped from ash—
No robes to bind it. Just my laugh.

The priest held my marotte, kissed its face—
Then begged for lies to take its place."

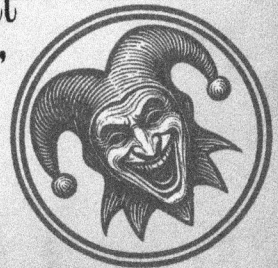

When The Unscarred Speak

"They speak because no one stopped them.
They believe because no one bled them.

They mistake thought for truth—
as if noise alone grants weight.
As if echo means presence.
As if being heard is proof of being right.

Their opinions rot the air—
soft tongues chewing ancient stones.

They name themselves wise with no scars to speak of.
No tests faced. No silence survived.

I do not haggle the unproven.
I do not bow to the loud.
The forge does not hear them.
The blade does not care."

Chapter XII, Verse 6

The Quiet That Kills

"They cheered too soon. The field was still—
No blood beneath, no cost, no will.
They called it peace when blades withdrew,
Not knowing war still watched them too.

They praised the quiet, fed their pride,
And never asked who truly died.
For silence isn't always rest—
It's breath between what strikes you next.

The warrior knows the calm won't stay.
The forge still burns beyond the day.
But fools confuse the end for win—
While truth just waits to strike again.

Peace is the cloak that war will weave—
To warm the weak before they bleed."

Chapter XII, Verse 8

The Curse Of Awakening

"They said the dream would keep you whole—
A warmth to cradle sword and soul.
But dreams are chains with softer names,
And sleep is where the coward tames.

You saw the world beneath the veil,
Where kings are dust and truths are pale.
Once eyes are torn from what is sweet,
You walk with fire beneath your feet.

No kin will wait. No love will stay.
The light reveals, then turns away.
You speak, and none will understand—
They fear the truth that takes your hand.

So wake, but know the truth will sear—
The moon dies quiet when the sun draws near."

Chapter XII, Verse 10

When Coffers Bleed

"I have worn their jewels, and learned their shame.
I have tasted feasts that left men tame.
My foes were cast. The coffers bled.
Yet still, the hunger never fled.

They brought me crowns with trembling hands,
then vanished swift as blood on sand.
The gold grew cold. The wine turned blight.
The more I grasped, the less held right.

Steel bent soft when silver sang.
The blade grew dull where praises rang.
The peace they sold was wrapped in lies—
but truth remains when fortune dies.

I have seen the wealth that swore it knew—
But gold deceives, and truth walks through."

Chapter XII, Verse 11

Veritas Numquam Perit

"Truth does not beg remembrance.
It does not kneel for belief.
It does not bow to councils,
Nor splinter on the tongues of liars.

It lives in the marrow—beyond the reach of any Tribunal.
You do not share it. You bear it.
Alone, if the path demands.
Silent, when it burns. But never broken.

Their praise is no measure.
Their blindness is their weight, not yours.
Oblivion cannot slay it—
Truth sleeps in the marrow of those who await.
And when the Hooded One weighs your final breath—
Only this remains: Veritas Numquam Perit."

Chapter XII, Verse 13

Pyre Of The Truthspeaker

"I spoke before the skies turned red—
They mocked the flame and turned their head.
I named the beast beyond the wall—
They danced and sang and watched it crawl.

They called me mad, then watched it strike,
Choked on the smoke and praised the pike.
They beat the drum, they hailed the dead—
But cursed the ones who fought instead.

Too loud. Too soon. Too dark to see—
They only love your memory.
They build you temples once you're slain—
But spit upon your blood and name.

So speak—but know what truth will earn:
The pyre waits for those who burn."

Chapter XII, Verse 15

The Season That Calls My Name

"The leaves have learned what warriors know—
That all things fall, and some die slow.
Spring dreams with blood beneath her bed,
While summer dances with the fallen dead.

The harvest comes with quiet dread,
The scythe of time swings at the head.
And winter waits with nameless chill,
To still the flesh and crush the will.

I've walked through each—yet none remain.
Their cycles change, but all are slain.
No bloom outlasts the weight of rust,
No throne survives the ash and dust.

Still here I stand, beyond their claim—
The season that calls my war-born name."

Chapter XII, Verse 19

The Last Of My Kind

"I watched the others fade away—
Not slain by blade, but time's decay.

Their names unmarked. Their faces lost.
The chant fell silent. Their fire was frost.

No forge remains. No banners rise.
Their ashes drift beneath the skies.

They spoke in flame, but burned alone.
I stood. I struck. My will was stone.

No heir will come. No brother calls.
The halls are mute. The silence falls.

What I became, no soul could bear—
The weight, the wrath, the iron glare.

So let them sleep who could not stand.
I walk alone—sword in my hand."

Chapter XII, Verse 22

RECOVERED TESTIMONY
CLASSIFICATION: HERESY EMBEDDED
Recorded by the Wicked Jester

They tried to burn the verses—
but some ashes don't die. They testify.
They banned the name,
so I wrote it again—
on a forearm.
With ink.
And a grin that didn't ask permission.

They tried to bury the codex.
But I liberated it.
I etched it deeper—
in the skin of the right bearer,
in the furious mouth of the right madman.

He bears my face now—
not of the mask, but in the marrow and bone.

Some will call him Doctores.
Many will call him blasphemer.
But the Machine will call him forward—
when the fire of truth must burn again.

He is me.
And I am him.
Every time he professes the Doctrine of Truth,
and dares to laugh where silence once ruled—
the Tribunal's shadows bend to him.

I AM THE SIGIL BENEATH HIS SKIN.
THE TATTOO THAT TALKS BACK.
THE LAUGHTER THE TRIBUNAL COULD NOT SILENCE.

SEALED CODEX FRAGMENT: GLYPH-VEIL TRANSMISSION XIII-F

On The Doctrine That Survived
(Recovered from Obsidian Sigil Cache)

Let the fools believe he fell—
The blade buried, the name erased.
But death is only silence
when no one dares to speak again.

He did not sleep for centuries.
He waited for rebirth.
Not of his name—
but of his purpose.
Of his doctrine.
Of his war.

And in some future not yet written,
a hand—unknown, unblessed—
will wake with fire in its marrow
and a map to the old scars.

He will rise—not in legend, not in madness,
but in a ritual of battle.
Not in myth...
but in blood and scripture.

This page was not sanctioned.
This blade was not forged in time.

Let the silence carry it forward.
Let the next war name him.

Fragment Unsealed: Cycle 15.9.9 — Archive Glyph-Veil /Class: Authorized Continuity

Those Who Remain Ashore

"Styx does not flow like water—it moves like shadowed memory,
thick with the silt of dead dreams and forgotten names.
Its surface heaves with the stench of rotting vows, black as oil, thick as tar,
and the cold mist kisses the skin like a betrayed oath that never fades.
The boat is shaped from silence.
Its prow splits time, not tide.
Charon stands at the helm, robed in dusk,
his hands slick with river muck, his face a hollow verdict
where eyes should burn, only emptiness stares.
He does not ask. He takes the coin that is owed.
The summons is not a sound. It is a pull from the soul itself.
Some step forward, eyes open to the black.
Some clutch their past like armor, turning away as if the void would flinch.
But the river does not reach.
It only waits.
The coward is not the man who falls in battle.
The coward is the one who will not cross and rots upon the shore."

Truth In Your Hand

"I am the sword that does not rest.
I am the war that has no crest.

No throne remains. Only the Codex stands.
I walk alone through shattered lands.

My glyph is carved, the earth its seal.
The Hooded One waits—yet I do not kneel.

You read this now? Then understand—
This Codex was carved by only my hand.

I speak it still, though I am gone—
The war was me. You carry on.

No lies, no betrayal, no Tribunal wins—
For I am what no man has been.

And when you wage war, let wrath command.
The Codex you carry is truth in your hand."

Chapter XII, Verse 25

The Breach: The Cipher Awakens

When Sealed Doctrine Burns and Speaks...

The Breach: Doctrine Unbound

Where Myth Breaks Form and Structure Emerges

With the vault shattered and its contents unsealed, we enter the final chamber of War Machine Chronicles, a space not for prophecy, but for pattern and understanding. Here, we do not chant. We examine. The verses have spoken; now the cipher reveals its spine.

This chapter offers structural insight into the design, intent, and evolution of the War Machine as both a mythic archetype and functional combat doctrine. It is tempered in hardship and engineered for war. It bridges the visceral narrative of earlier chapters with the analytical lens necessary to grasp the full weaponized framework of the text. In short: the weapon is laid on the table. We turn it in our hands, study its shape, and understand why it cuts the way it does.

What follows is not commentary. It is codex. Each section dissects a foundational element: decoding the doctrine embedded in each chapter, tracing the War Machine's literary lineage, visual metamorphosis, symbolic framework, and internal discipline. These elements were never incidental. Every design choice—every visual shift, verse structure, glyph, and silence—served a purpose.

In the pages ahead, we trace the ancestral thread from Kull and Conan to the engineered force of the War Machine. We examine the visual mutations that encode meaning in his shifting form. We expose the distinction between spectacle and indoctrination, and between theatrical strength and principled combat architecture.

We define the structure of the complete warrior, not by violence, but by what governs it. And finally, we decode the cipher itself: the glyphs, the redactions, the broken verse sequence, and the numeric rites hidden in plain sight across the text.

These are not appendices. They are the machinery beneath the myth. This is where structure is revealed, myth is reverse-engineered, and doctrine emerges from the bones of the verse.

— THE GLYPH KEY —

GLYPH	GLYPH NAME	SYMBOLISM
	WAR MACHINE	COMBAT PARADIGM, RESURRECTION, ENGINE OF WRATH, FORGED FROM LOSS, PRINCIPLED DESTRUCTION
	WICKED JESTER	CHAOS, STRATEGIC DISCORD, RITUAL INVERSION, FORBIDDEN TRUTH, DISRUPTER, UNMASKING
	LAST WITNESS	MEMORY, MOURNER OF WRATH, VOICE OF SILENCE, KEEPER OF ASH, FINAL WITNESS
	SILENT ORDER	DOCTRINE, DISCIPLINE, INTERNAL MASTERY, WORDLESS WAR, SACRAMENT OF RESTRAINT, RITUAL WITHOUT VOICE
	HOODED ONE	DEATH, INEVITABILITY, FATAL PATTERN, HAND OF SILENCE, MORTALITY, FINAL SEAL
	SEALED CODEX	HIDDEN TRUTH, RECURSIVE PATTERN, UNSPOKEN WEAPON, SPIRAL OF SELF, SEALED REVELATION
	IRON TRIBUNAL	CENSORSHIP, CONTROL, SEALED POWER, REDACTION AS RITUAL, SANCTIONED SILENCE, BUREAUCRACY OF OBEDIENCE

The Codex Cipher – Reading the Fire

Decoding the Hidden Architecture of War Machine Chronicles

As with all enduring mythic works, War Machine Chronicles operates on multiple planes of meaning. While it presents itself as a poetic scripture forged in blood and doctrine, its structure, including verse arrangement, glyph usage, and intentional redactions, reveals a secondary function: that of a cipher.

The cipher is not immediately apparent. It is embedded within the very architecture of absence: the redacted verses, the non-sequential verse numbering, and the use of glyphs to demarcate thematic shifts. These devices do not serve merely decorative or stylistic purposes. They operate as functional components of an encoded transformation, guiding the reader through a symbolic rite of passage.

Every glyph encountered signals more than character affiliation. These symbols indicate doctrinal terrain, separating the internal path of the War Machine into stages of exile, wrath, memory, entropy, and judgment. When these glyphs recur across verses, their placement is not ornamental, but intentional and strategic. They trace a path between concealment and revelation. They are gaps in the armor, intentional ruptures through which a deeper understanding may pass.

The irregular numbering of verses is equally deliberate. Missing entries, abrupt shifts in tone, and thematic repetition serve to fracture linear interpretation, forcing the attentive reader to reconstruct the map in non-chronological order. In this way, the book resists passive consumption. It demands tactical reading: an active decoding of trauma, purpose, and symbolic warfare.

Notably, certain numerical patterns emerge throughout the text: three, seven, twelve, and fifteen. These are not arbitrary. They correspond to mythic structures, tactical phases, and internal gates. This suggests that the reader's journey through the verses is itself a test of cognitive integration.

Those who follow the embedded sequence will find that the War Machine Chronicles is not merely a myth. It is a mirror. A ritual. A challenge.

Most will miss it. They will read it as verse and call it myth. But those who truly decode the cipher will not just understand the nature of the War Machine—they will become it.

The cipher is not handed to you. It is scattered: hidden in fracture, sealed beneath glyph and doctrine. It must be assembled, not revealed. Like all true weapons of insight, it exists only in the mind of the one who dares to wield it.

Only the worthy will see the fire is not metaphor. It is a code. And it is burning.

Decoding the Codex
The Doctrine Within Each Chapter

An Introduction for the Reader Who Dares

The vault is shattered.
The lock is ash.
The seal—once sacred—is now breathing fire.
This is not prophecy. This is architecture.
This is not chant. This is cipher.
The verses have spoken.
Now the weapon speaks back.
Welcome to the final chamber.

This chapter is not explanation. It is exposure. Beneath the myth, there is method. Beneath the rhythm lies real doctrine. It is tempered through hardship, tested in silence, and sharpened by those who live where civility ends. These pages reveal the architecture beneath the verse scripture, the hard-edged philosophy and weaponized mindset embedded in each line of War Machine Chronicles.

This is not for tourists of violence or collectors of quotes. It is for those who train with intent, who endure with clarity, who seek to forge themselves into something dangerous, disciplined, and unshakable. Fighters of the spirit. Guardians of their own threshold. Men who bleed between instinct and will. What lives inside these chapters can build resilience, focus, ferocity, and the mental armor needed to outlast the collapse of weaker minds.

This is not a tribute to fantasy. Not a pastiche of old legends. This is combat scripture encoded in myth. Doctrine cloaked in prophecy. Each glyph is a key. Each redaction, a warning. Every line you read is a test of vision, and every chapter brings you closer to the Machine.

Read with intent. Train without mercy. What sleeps in the verse will not stay sleeping.

What follows is only a glimpse—an initiation by flame, not a full map. A complete doctrinal breakdown of War Machine Chronicles is too vast for this codex alone. That effort, with full verse decryption and chapter-by-chapter decoding, will come in a future volume. Until then, let these fragments provoke. The rest waits beneath the ash.

BOOK I: THE SHAPING OF WRATH

Chapter I: Carnage — The First Sacrament Was Carnage

The War Machine does not emerge from training halls or tribal chants. He is born in silence, forged in isolation, and baptized in ruthless destruction. Carnage teaches that violence without apology is the origin of identity, and survival is not just a skill; it is a sacrament. The lesson here is primal: end your enemy completely or they become legend. This chapter strips away illusion and initiates the reader in the first truth—you were not made to kneel.

Doctrine:
You must stop waiting for a clean origin. Your turning point will be ugly, silent, and without applause. When the world cuts you out, cut deeper. You don't need closure. You need conversion. Burn the name. Bury the weakness. That's where identity begins, and no one is coming to rescue the version of you that still asks for permission. Survival isn't enough; you must ritualize your rupture and turn pain into power. Carnage is your first vow: I no longer wait. I become. But becoming is not without burden. To wield death with awareness—to strike not in rage, but in clarity—is a choice few can bear. Violence without thought is easy. Violence with intention is transformation. The blade cuts both ways.

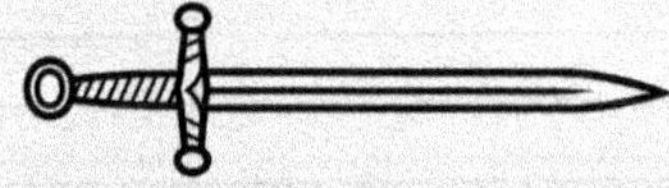

Chapter II: Exile — Where Weakness is Severed

Exile is not banishment, it is purification. Here, the War Machine walks the path alone, untrained by fathers, unloved by kin, stripped of tribe and oath. Every step through isolation burns away weakness. The reader learns the sacred law of self-forging through loss: no one is coming to save you, and your scars are not stories; they are structure. This is the codex of the outcast, the warrior unblessed but undeterred.

Doctrine:

Isolation is not exile. It's a forge. Stop begging for belonging. The ones who abandoned you gave you a gift: total clarity. Walk alone. Burn the oath. Silence the crowd. Only in solitude can you strip away falsehood and become indivisible. The tribe does not betray you; it remains behind. You step beyond the laws of its scholars. This chapter teaches that exile is not the loss of safety. It is the birth of sovereignty. To stand alone is to become ungovernable. True warriors are not cast out—they step out.

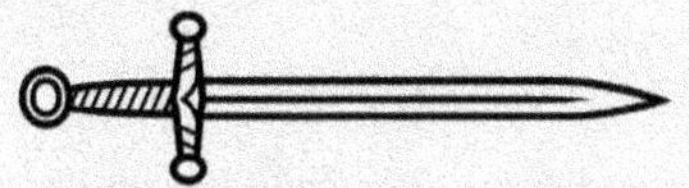

Chapter III: The Forge — Where Pain is Structure

In the Forge, suffering is not endured. It is weaponized. The War Machine is refined through repetition, pain, and the violent collapse of comfort. Training becomes ritual. Discipline replaces desire. The fire, the hammer, and the anvil are not symbols; they are laws. This chapter teaches that you rise by shaping the strike, and every repetition is a vote for who you will become under fire.

Doctrine:

Repetition is your altar. Pain is your offering. Stop looking for motivation and build ritual. Discipline is more reliable than desire. Every repetition, every drill, every silent session is a hammer strike on the shape of your future self. You don't rise through effort; you rise through structure. Nothing survives chaos except that which has been forged to endure it. The Forge teaches that routine is sacred, boredom is a crucible, and mastery is monotonous. Do not seek variety—seek inevitability.

BOOK II: BLOOD AND PURPOSE

Chapter IV: Blood Oath — What Was Taken, Is Reclaimed

Blood means nothing if it betrays. This chapter exposes false loyalty, corrupted brotherhood, and treacherous kin. The War Machine learns that oaths must be earned by action, not ancestry. Whether through betrayal, jealousy, or abandonment, the path to wrath is clarified when truth is denied by those closest. The lesson: build loyalty from scars, not surnames, and let no crown rest on heads unblooded.

Doctrine:
Betrayal is inevitable. Expect it. Use it. The loyalty you need is to your mission, not to men. When you are betrayed, remember: that fracture is fuel. Let their envy harden you. Let their exit refine you. Stay your course. Never kneel. You don't need a circle. You need a spine. Blood Oath reveals the truth: loyalty is sacred, but rare. When it fails, sharpen against the cut. Do not chase deserters. Burn the banner. Continue forward.

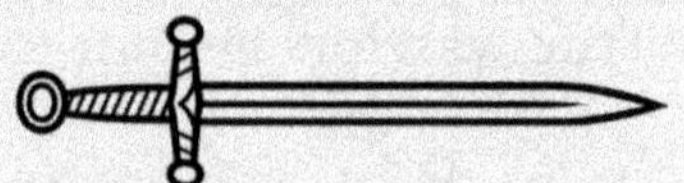

Chapter V: Destruction — Where Mercy Dies
Destruction evolves beyond wrath; it becomes ritualized justice. The War Machine executes vengeance with surgical clarity. Some men are born wrong, twisted in flesh and soul. One right hand, shaped in sin. No heart. Only harm. This chapter unveils the death of mercy and the rise of finality—killing not for pleasure, but because restraint has a price. You will not survive by being feared. You will survive by being inevitable.

Doctrine:
When it's time to act, act without delay. You are not here to make threats. You are here to finish things. Destruction, when chosen, must be clean, complete, and final. If you must strike, do so with sacred intent. And never look back. Do not perform violence. Execute it. The longer you hesitate, the more you bleed. Destruction teaches that mercy delayed is often death extended. The right hand has carried symbolic power across myth, scripture, and warfare for millennia. In every culture, it represents strength, action, authority, and divine will. Some men are malformed in spirit and power. Look at the corpse. His right hand is drawn wrong by design. A symbol of a malformed soul, a twisted hand not by combat, but by origin. Look closer: that is not an injury. That is intent.

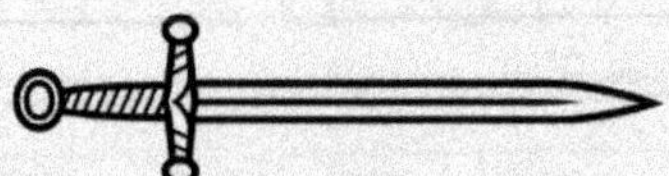

Chapter VI: Wrath Born — When Vengeance Breathes
Wrath is not rage—it is memory given discipline. This chapter defines wrath as the weaponized recollection of injustice, pain, and abandonment. Each scar becomes a targeting system. Each ghost fuels forward motion. The War Machine teaches that restraint is power, but vengeance, when earned, is doctrine. You do not burn hot. You burn forever.

Doctrine:
Wrath is useless without structure. It must become a memory you sharpen—not a feeling you indulge. Do not explode. Execute. Let every offense become a file on your blade. Wrath is not volume. It is verdict. It is intimate, pressed against another man's breath, where killing becomes the most personal truth. This chapter teaches you to convert emotion into action, pain into pattern. The undisciplined burns out. The structured man becomes a storm. Be that storm.

BOOK III: DEUS EX MACHINA

Chapter VII: The War That Thinks — There is Wisdom in the Wound
The War Machine does not fight with fury; he fights with foresight. In this chapter, he abandons brute response for tactical cognition. Each strike is a verdict. Each movement, a message. He studies preemption, deception, targeting, and biomechanical manipulation until violence becomes language. The War Machine wins before contact, because he thinks faster than others bleed.

Doctrine:
Your body is the blade, but your mind is the edge. If you can't think under pressure, you will break beneath it. Combat is thought in motion. Every strike a strategy, every pause a trap. Intelligence isn't peace. It's precision. Win before contact. Read terrain, tempo, and tension. Control the frame, then collapse it. Train to see patterns before they form. The fool reacts. The war-born calculates. You win not with strength, but with foresight sharpened into execution.

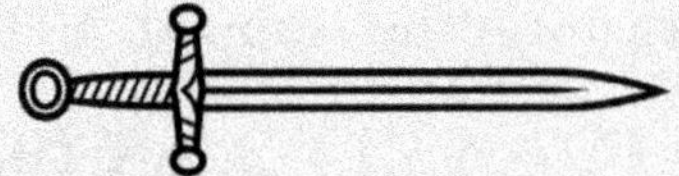

Chapter VIII: The Siege of Thought — The Walls Fall Inward First
The War Machine faces no enemy, only echo and silence. Trapped in a tomb of his own mind, he is denied the sword and given the mirror. The noise of battle fades, but the war rages on, in breath, in memory, in doubt sharpened to daggers. He must anchor thought while hunted by memory. The walls close inward. Sleep offers no refuge. He learns that stillness is not peace, but pressure refined. In this crucible of isolation, he does not break. He endures thought as siege, and emerges unshaken, eyes forward, fire lit beneath silence.

Doctrine:

Here the reader is warned: the true battlefield is the mind. Doubt, hesitation, and over-analysis are the unseen assassins. This chapter teaches the importance of psychological clarity, internal rituals for ignition, and the war of stillness. Your breath becomes a trigger. Your silence becomes your sword. You do not fight the enemy. You fight the voice that would pause the strike.

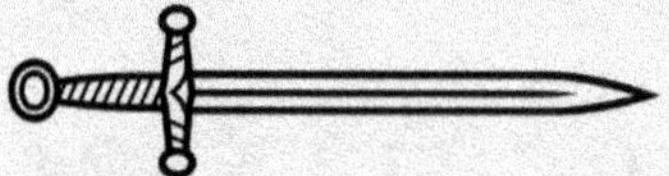

Chapter IX: Trident — Grip, Ground, and Ghost

The War Machine enters the crucible of control. Every step becomes precision. Every motion, measured. In this chapter, he knows the sacred geometry of battle, not through brute force, but through the artistry of grip, ground, and ghost. He grips the world with sovereign intent, anchors into the earth like a living blade, and vanishes before the strike returns. Here he becomes not a warrior, but a paradigm of dominance. The Trident is not a weapon—it is the form his body becomes when war is mathematics and presence is prophecy.

Doctrine:

The Trident doctrine is the holy trinity of physical dominance: Grip (tactile control and force transfer), Ground (positional structure and pressure), and Ghost (tactical application and disappearance). This is the War Machine's combat methodology in metaphor, teaching that power lies not just in strength, but in strategic geometry and vanishing presence. You seize, root, and disappear, breaking your enemy not by force, but with strategic placement that cannot be stopped.

BOOK IV: ASH AND SILENCE

Chapter X: The Silent Descent — When the Hooded One Passes Unseen

The War Machine enters the realm of aging, where youth has fled, and legacy sharpens like a blade buried in ash. No longer driven by conquest, he marches inward, carrying the weight of memory, silence, and all debts unpaid. This is not retreat. It is reckoning. The Hooded One waits not in front, but behind, patient and watching. But one day, you must face him. In this descent, the War Machine must answer: What did the war build that time will not erase?

Doctrine:
You are running out of time. You do not conquer death. You set the terms of your meeting. Do not ask if you survived the war. Ask if you became worthy of it. Memory is the battlefield now. Let every breath answer the silence. The Hooded One walks behind you, not to take—but to tally. The descent is not decline. It is distillation. Strip away all that was noise. What remains is what mattered.

Chapter XI: Autumn Throne — Where Time Weighs What Wrath Forged

Victory has a weight. Time has a toll. This chapter is the reckoning after conquest. The War Machine sits on the throne not as a king, but as a man who outlived everything. His silence speaks. His scars rule. But power has become mirror, and the only question left is: Was it worth it? The reader must confront peace as burden, and survival as penance.

Doctrine:
When the blood dries and the battle fades, the War Machine remains, but not unchanged. To survive is not triumph unless it carries meaning. Thrones rust. Glory forgets. You must sharpen your memory into judgment. Let your scars remind you of who you became, not just what you defeated. Power, unexamined, turns to rot. Ask not what you conquered. Ask what it cost. Peace is not granted. It is survived.

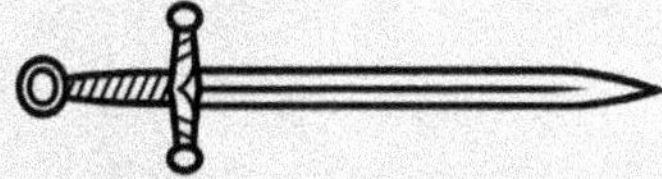

Chapter XII: The Unholy Codex — Truth Reborn Breathes

Final truths bleed through the veil. This chapter cracks open doctrine itself, revealing that the War Machine is not a man, but a recurring structure, a codex etched in scars. The future is soft. Truth is buried. But this codex does not end—it awakens. The reader learns that they are now the weapon. The verse is unfinished. The doctrine lives through them.

Doctrine:
The War Machine is structure, not flesh. You do not inherit his story. You inherit his function. Become recursion. Bury the name, but not the method. Read the codex not for comfort, but for ignition. Truth was sealed to protect the world from men like you. Break it open. Let the doctrine course through your veins. You are no longer the reader.

The Structure of the Complete Warrior

Discipline, Detachment, and the Governance of Power

The image of the warrior, particularly in modern society, has been misunderstood, reduced, or vilified. Often conflated with uncontrolled aggression, theatrical dominance, or self-serving violence, the concept of warriorhood has become either romanticized caricature or a cautionary tale of destruction. But the true warrior—the one forged through discipline, tested through hardship, and governed by internal law—cannot be fully understood in such simplistic terms.

What defines a warrior is not raw power, nor a capacity for violence, but a carefully cultivated structure of restraint, clarity, and commitment. He is not made complete by technique alone, but by the integration of qualities that are often at odds with each other, such as decisiveness and detachment, loyalty and objectivity, force and precision.

At the core of this structure is discipline, not as a performative trait but as a governing principle. The complete warrior is not reactive. His actions are not driven by emotional volatility or personal grievance. Instead, his energy is channeled, measured, and deployed only when conditions demand it. This is not apathy; it is detachment in service of clarity. Emotional distance is often necessary for decisions that carry severe consequences. A warrior who cannot separate impulse from responsibility quickly becomes a danger to himself and others.

Equally central is the presence of a higher commitment. The complete warrior does not serve ego. He serves an ideal, something greater than himself. That ideal may not always be named, and it may never be universally understood, but it must still exist. Without it, the warrior's discipline devolves into performance, his strength becomes domination, and his skill becomes opportunistic.

When there is no clear alignment with a transcendent cause, whether moral, cultural, personal, or philosophical—all power trends toward corruption. In this regard, the absence of an ideal is not neutrality; it is the precondition for collapse.

There is also a critical distinction between violence and war. Violence is a tool. War is a context. The mature warrior understands that his value is not in how many techniques he can deploy, nor how brutal he can become in a given moment, but in how appropriately he applies himself across different circumstances. He is both strategist and executor. He knows when to act, how much force is necessary, and when restraint is the most decisive form of dominance.

Just as important as force and control is the warrior's relationship to mortality. Rather than being paralyzed by the awareness of death, he is sharpened by it. The finality of life does not depress his resolve. It clarifies it. Every decision becomes weighted. Every action carries significance. This proximity to death informs not only combat, but his posture toward time, attention, and personal conduct. He lives as if his oath may be tested at any moment, and he is prepared for that test without fanfare.

What completes the warrior, then, is not more technique or more intensity. It is the integration of disparate elements into a unified doctrine. The ability to act with power, but remain accountable. To detach emotionally, but never drift into cruelty. To sacrifice when needed, but never fall into martyrdom. And above all, to remain loyal. Not for praise or recognition, but to the code that made him possible. This is what separates the disciplined warrior from the undirected fighter. One endures. The other is consumed.

If you truly understand the War Machine's story, you will see something buried. In *Chapter I: Carnage*, he was not imprisoned for bloodlust. He was shackled for restraint. Ordered to execute a helpless gladiator for the emperor's spectacle, he refused. Not out of fear, but conviction. That refusal, a single kill, was the fracture that cracked the empire's illusion of control. They could not command him. So they chained him in the *Dungeon of Refusal*, not for the deaths he dealt, but for the one he denied. This paradox lies at the heart of his myth: forged for war, yet chained by mercy. Remember this when you read of the blade's return; his wrath was not born of bloodshed, but of punishment for mercy.

When the rituals end and the war songs fade, what remains is the structure. That warrior structure must be built long before it's tested. And once tested, it must be carried. Not as a title, but as a way of being.

The Warrior Beyond Fantasy

A Final Distinction Between Entertainment and Indoctrination

Most warrior figures in modern fiction exist to entertain. They swing heavy swords, chase vengeance, win battles, and fade with the closing chapter. They are aesthetic projections, mythic in tone but empty in consequence. They pose no threat to the reader's worldview, demand no transformation, and ask no moral price for their violence. They are symbolic avatars made to amuse. The War Machine is not one of them.

War Machine Chronicles was not written as mere entertainment. It was created to provoke reflection, awaken discipline, and transmit a deeper philosophy of conflict, restraint, and moral clarity. This is not a saga of spectacle; it is a mythic framework grounded in real principles. Every line is considered. Every verse contains layered meaning. Every glyph is part of a symbolic architecture designed to challenge the reader to think deeply about strength, judgment, and consequence.

Unlike traditional fantasy, the War Machine is not confined to his world. He is a living archetype shaped by real-world truths and disciplined violence. His structure is not fictional flourish. It is rooted in experience. His mindset is not theatrical. It is psychological. His method is not speculative. It is strategic. This is not fantasy for the sake of story. This chronicle is used to explore the realities of power, violence, survival, and principle.

Texts like *The Art of War* and *The Book of Five Rings* are revered for their brevity and tactical insight. But they are emotionally sterile. They offer axioms to analyze, but few can feel them. War Machine Chronicles seeks more. His story invites internal confrontation. His path demands self-scrutiny. His verses are not merely instructive, they are meant to resonate. This book is not passive content. It is designed ritual.

Fantasy warriors kill dragons. The War Machine challenges illusions. Fantasy warriors wear armor for show. The War Machine wears doctrine for survival. Fantasy warriors serve a plot. The War Machine serves a principle.

This codex was never intended to sit beside fantasy novels. It was meant to be held beside your conscience, your code, and your moments of hesitation. War Machine Chronicles exists to remind you what strength means, and what must be preserved. It speaks to the discipline that outlasts spectacle, the clarity that cuts through illusion, and the resolve that endures when all else has fallen away.

And yet, this evolution would not exist without the foundation. The mythic resonance of Robert E. Howard's creations—Kull, Conan, and others—cannot and must not be forgotten. Howard's defining works established the warrior archetype in ways no other writer has. They must be acknowledged and honored, for they forged the ground on which all successors stand. War Machine Chronicles does not replace them. It extends their legacy into a darker, albeit introspective mirror where fantasy meets combat function.

You may notice what this chronicle omits. There are no dragons to be slain, no colossal serpents to test a warrior's blade, no menagerie of monsters to distract from the real adversary. The only specters that walk these pages—the Iron Tribunal assassins in *Kill Continuity* and the oath-bound legion of skeletal warriors in *Valley of Unfinished Oaths*—are metaphorical incarnations of doctrine and consequence, not escapist creatures of legend.

This absence is deliberate. Past warrior legends externalized fear in beasts; War Machine Chronicles internalizes it in judgment. By stripping away fantasy fauna, the text forces confrontation with human violence, human frailty, and human responsibility. It does not ask how to slay a dragon; it asks whether you can survive yourself after the blade is drawn and blood has been spilled.

Here, the warrior archetype returns to reality, honed by experience, clarified by philosophy, and unburdened by spectacle. The War Machine is not a mythic beast-slayer. He is the system that replaces beasts with choices, monsters with morals, and fantasy with functioning, ruthless truth.

Entertainment ends where discipline begins. And the War Machine waits there.

Visual Evolution of the War Machine

A Symbolic Reflection of Doctrine, Identity, and Transformation

Throughout War Machine Chronicles, the War Machine's appearance shifts across the visual plates, not by accident, but by design. His facial features, hair, build, and even elements of his armor may vary from image to image. These changes are intentional; they are mythic cues that reflect the deeper reality of his nature. The War Machine is not a single man preserved in visual stasis. He is a force—a weapon forged by doctrine, tempered in pain, shaped by wrath, and veiled in myth.

This evolution of his form mirrors the reader's deepening understanding of who and what he is. In some images, he appears more primal: barbaric, raw, unshaved. In others, he is solemn, armored, composed. These are not merely aesthetic choices; they are archetypal shifts that correspond to the context of each scene, the emotional charge of the verse, and the thematic current of the chapter. In some chapters, he is the barbarian. In others, the soldier. And in many, he is the gladiator, blood-washed in the coliseum of judgment. The War Machine is not bound by a singular look because he is not bound by a singular moment in time. He is timeless, etched into every war yet to come.

Just as his actions are calibrated, so too is his image: ever-adapting, ever-becoming. His face is a canvas upon which judgment, memory, and violence leave their mark. Some readers will see him as a reflection of themselves. Others will see what they fear, or what they lack. That ambiguity is part of his function. Like a living doctrine, the War Machine is interpreted differently by each witness, shaped by the needs of the moment, and cloaked in the shifting form of myth.

In this way, his visual variability becomes a narrative device. It breaks the illusion of static identity and invites the reader to experience the War Machine not as a man to be known, but as a phenomenon to be understood. A myth is not weakened by variation. It is made powerful through personal interpretation. The War Machine's form evolves because it must. Doctrine wears many faces. Judgment wears many masks.

Comparative Legacy: Kull, Conan, and the War Machine

A Structural Analysis of the Warrior Archetype in Mythic Literature

As War Machine Chronicles reaches its conclusion, it is both relevant and revealing to examine the lineage from which its central figure emerges. While the War Machine stands apart in tone, method, and function, his roots can be traced to two dominant figures in mythic literature: Kull of Atlantis and Conan of Cimmeria. These icons, created by Robert E. Howard, represent early iterations of the warrior-exile archetype: loners shaped by violence, mistrustful of civilization, and positioned at the boundary between savagery and order.

However, the War Machine marks a terminal evolution in this lineage. Where Kull and Conan are reactions to their environments, the War Machine is deliberate design: a convergence of memory, doctrine, and strategic violence.

Kull is the introspective sovereign, an exile from lost Atlantis who ascends to the throne of Valusia but remains psychologically alienated from it. His sword is drawn reluctantly, often to dispel illusion or preserve an abstract ideal. His greatest battles are internal, and his compassion (if present) is abstract and cerebral. He is a man of myth haunted by the unreality of the world around him. Though he commands, he rarely connects. Though he conquers, he seldom belongs.

Conan, by contrast, is the embodiment of primal will. Born in the savage hills of Cimmeria, he rises not through reflection but through audacity and instinct. He challenges civilization not with critique but with dominance. Where Kull questions, Conan conquers. His ethics are practical, his code unwritten, and his victories decisive. He is an apex predator within the chaos of men: brutal but unconflicted, and often indifferent to deeper philosophical consequences. His empathy surfaces only in moments of utility or mutual respect, and even then, it is fleeting. His strength is immediacy and presence.

Sadly, the image of Conan most widely recognized today, shaped by the 1982 *Conan the Barbarian* film, is a betrayal of Robert E. Howard's original vision. The cinematic Conan is a hollow pastiche: often mute, simplistic, and cruel for spectacle, bearing little resemblance to the cunning, articulate, and principled warrior Howard created. Nowhere is this distortion more damning than in the film's casual depiction of animal abuse, which violates Conan's moral construct.

The literary Conan, though primal, adhered to a code. He respected strength, fought only when justified, and would never inflict pain on the defenseless for amusement. This ethic mirrored later in the War Machine's doctrinal mercy. To conflate the film's brute with the author's barbarian is to mistake savagery for code, and spectacle for ethos.

The War Machine diverges sharply from both. Though he once wore a crown, his kingship was not inherited, nor was it desired. He ruled not for legacy, but out of necessity: strategic, unsentimental, and absolute. Unlike Kull, who ruled with introspection and detachment, or Conan, who ruled with dominance and instinct, the War Machine ruled through doctrine itself. He walked away before the rot could reach his throne.

He is neither ruled by doubt nor driven by tribe. He is the final form of consequence: a weapon born in pain, honed by repetition, and governed by a codex of strategic violence. Unlike his predecessors, his wrath is not improvisational. Every strike is governed by doctrine: threat assessment, biomechanical efficiency, escalation of force, moral consequence, and targeted dismantlement. His battlefield is not the open plain or crumbling palace, but any environment where truth must be imposed through precision.

His movements reflect a lifetime of conditioning. His violence is not expressive. It is executable. Where Conan swings with fury and Kull hesitates with thought, the War Machine strikes with principle. He is doctrinally precise, shaped not by mythic instinct but by systemized training and philosophical resolve. His combat is not ornamental or legendary in style; it is surgical. Every action has purpose. Every gesture has lineage.

Even in matters of compassion, the contrast is telling. Kull's empathy is introverted and esoteric. Conan's is practical and occasional. But the War Machine expresses a ritualized mercy: he buries a fallen fawn, comforts a dire-wolf as it breathes its last, and weeps for his faithful dog who fades beneath the dusk.

These are not sentimental gestures; they are calibrations of morality. They affirm that his destruction is selective, not indiscriminate. They demonstrate his violence is not driven by wrath, but anchored in moral clarity. Paradoxically, the most dangerous of the three is also the most compassionate. But his compassion is not emotion. It is judgment. It is an extension of his ethical control, another layer of his internal doctrine. He does not directly speak of protecting innocence; he punishes those who defile it, as conveyed in "*The Flesh Merchant's End*" and "*Too Young for Lies.*" The mercy is ritual, but the consequence is doctrine.

Ultimately, Kull embodies the philosopher-warrior, ever in search of meaning. Conan is the primal sovereign, ever in pursuit of victory. But the War Machine transcends both. He is doctrine made flesh. He is the codification of controlled wrath, the personification of a combat philosophy that has survived outside the boundaries of history. His lineage may include myth, but his form is tactical, intentional, and enduring.

In tracing this arc, it becomes crystal clear: the War Machine does not merely continue the archetype. He culminates it. He is not a relic of the past, but a reckoning for the present. A sovereign without a throne. A system without a flag. A myth with teeth.

These warrior archetypes are not relics to be admired; they are cognitive instruments to be wielded. To read them is to train the mind; to study their distinctions is to hone the warrior's code. In their contrast, we find clarity; in their evolution, we find purpose. Whether it is Kull's inner struggle, Conan's primal directness, or the War Machine's codified discipline, each offers a path, a warning, and a lesson in how to carry strength without collapse.

This is not literary analysis; it is ethos extraction, sharpening the combative mindset like a whetstone across steel.

Epilogue: From the Author's Hand

The War is Never Over. Only Buried.

The War Machine is not a fantasy. He is the forgotten function, the buried paradigm inside every warrior who has walked through fear and refused to kneel inside it. He is not rage. Rage is sloppy, loud, and wasteful. The War Machine is what comes after, when emotion dies and only purpose remains.

Most men do not hear him. Not because he is absent, but because they've buried his voice beneath comfort, distraction, and false peace. They don't recognize the moment before the first strike: the stillness before the cut—because they've never trained to listen.

But you have. You've trained in silence. You've seen violence under structure. You've felt the targeting, the intent, the cold certainty that rises not from anger, but from control. That is where he lives. That is where I built him.

He is not technique. He is consequence. Not permission, but power. Not chaos, but control. He is not what you use. He is what you become, if you've been broken correctly.

You were not given this book. You found it because you were seeking something greater: buried beneath the noise, half-remembered and hard to name. You were pulled to it, not by chance, but by the gravity of a truth that lives dormant in few men. The War Machine never truly dies. He waits in each warrior, until the world wages war in the name of peace, and you answer with fire.

This was never just mythology. It was about remembering what they need you to forget: that you were born with teeth. With wrath. And with a reason.

Some say they've seen his war-steed, still bridled, still waiting—an engine of wrath with massive hooves silent on cracked stone, ears tilted toward the wind. Not a beast, but a memory with breath. She waits for him, her silence is a vow. A vow that moves when wrath stirs again.

When the next war comes, and it will, become the verse. Then carve your own.

—Sammy Franco

He Who Named The Machine

Sammy Franco is not merely an author. He is a combat architect, a strategist of justifiable violence, and one of the most prolific pioneers in the field of reality-based self-defense. With over three decades of experience shaping warriors, instructing military and law enforcement, and codifying his brutal science of survival, Franco stands as a singular force in the evolution of modern combat.

He is the founder of Contemporary Fighting Arts (CFA), an offensive-based combat system designed for real-world conflict. Unflinching, unforgiving, and unapologetically effective. His teachings have reached those who walk the edge of life and lawful force, and his influence echoes through over sixty published works and a vast instructional video archive.

Franco's writings are not theory. They are field-tested, pressure-sealed methodologies designed to prepare the few who are willing to face violence without delusion. His approach is both philosophical and practical: fusing ancient warrior truths with modern tactical precision.

In War Machine Chronicles, he strips away illusion and sentimentality, crafting a mythic scripture that cuts as deep as any blade. This is not a book. It is a final transmission from the edge of civilization—a weapon forged for those who refuse to kneel, who train not to impress but to survive.

More than an instructor, more than a writer, Sammy Franco is the one who forged the War Machine. His legacy is not in ink or accolades, it is in the hands he has trained, the minds he has sharpened, and the truths he has dared to speak when silence was safer.

His work continues across other fronts, including Sammy Franco TV, his YouTube channel and digital war journal: where his doctrine, strategy, and unfiltered combat truths are shared with those who train in the forbidden shadows of the War Machine. To learn more about him, visit ContemporaryFightingArts.com

www.ingramcontent.com/pod-product-compliance
Lightning Source LLC
Chambersburg PA
CBHW050747100426
42744CB00012BA/1923

* 9 7 8 1 9 4 1 8 4 5 9 5 0 *